MW01253674

Two things separate Anne from all other people I have met, the depth of the suffering she endured in her early life, and her faith in Christ. It is a marker of her closeness to God that peace and joy dominate this book. Although terrible trauma and anguish dominated her early life, faith hope and love have ultimately triumphed.

Dr. Eric Kuelker, R.Psych.

While at times painful to digest, *The Air I Breathe* never ceases to impel you toward a deeper understanding of who you are. Its broader scope is refreshing and challenging as well, moving beyond personal healing to emphasize reliance on God and humble service to others. Throughout, Koltes sensitively articulates the defeatist thoughts, pent up feelings and toxic emotions that she has experienced, but have perhaps struggled to put into words – until now. With the practical strategies outlined in these pages, you too will learn to give voice to your innermost pain and find new meaning and purpose in each breath you take.

Cara Plett, BA English
Christian Marriage & Parenting Writer

THE AIR I
BREATHE

THE AIR I BREATHE

A Journey Towards Healing

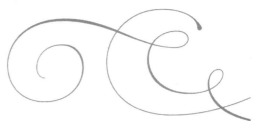

ANNE A. KOLTES

THE AIR I BREATHE
Copyright © 2014 by Anne A. Koltes

Printed In Canada

ISBN: 978-1-4866-0238-4

Word Alive Press
131 Cordite Road, Winnipeg, MB R3W 1S1
www.wordalivepress.ca

	MIX
FSC www.fsc.org	Paper from responsible sources FSC® C016245

Cataloguing in Publication may be obtained through Library and Archives Canada

Contents

In Appreciation...

(It's the Bumps in the Road That Teach
Us Along Our Life's Journey)

I dedicate this book to my first love, the most important one in my life, my Lord and Savior, Jesus Christ. He has been by my side through all my darkness, tears, hurt, pain, joy and laughter. When I thought no one was really there, He carried me and dried my tears. I am breathing today because of His love for me.

I also dedicate this book to my husband, Richard, who has been caring, kind, steadfast, supportive and faithful, showing his love through each step of the way. I also dedicate this book to all seven of our precious adult children, whom God has given me such a deep love for, and to my adoptive parents, brothers, and sisters, who were chosen for me by the Lord, picked out especially for me! My prayer for each of you is that you search your heart and find the love God has given you to follow His ways each day.

A special thanks to my doctors and counselors that the Lord has led me to in the process of my healing. You have been encouraging and helpful. Thank you.

May you never doubt that the air you breathe is yours. It is God's gift to you. He loves you!

Preface

Do you ever feel like you do not deserve the air you are breathing? That you are not valued and do not belong in this world? Do you feel that you are breathing someone else's air, and it's not really yours? In other words, you feel like a stranger on this earth. Life just seems too tough, and you are very weary; your strength is just hanging on by a small thread!

You may not have confidence, due to others' negative behavior towards you. If you have never been cared for, loved and valued while growing up, these are the types of feelings that may arise. If left alone and not dealt with in a positive manner, they can become toxic.

I felt this way for most of my life, because of having no positive validation in my young life and tremendous struggles thus far. Then I began with God's help and guidance to walk down the road to recovery.

You may say, "I don't know how to change the way I feel inside." The first thing you need to know is, you cannot do it alone. God can help you as you look unto Him humbly for direction, strength and grace. As you seek God, He can lead you to good support groups and counseling that are very helpful, and you will find that you are not alone. Ask God to help you find a few caring people who can offer you strength and encouragement while you embark upon this most difficult path in your journey to recovery.

It is never easy to change and let go of toxic things that linger deep within us from dark trials we have experienced. If we continue to hang on to these toxins in our lives, the weight will continue to pull us down, and eventually depression can set in. Giving our trials and hurts to God while learning the healthy tools needed to become free of the toxins that have piled up within us throughout the years will free us so we can enjoy a healthy life. Then we will be able to engage in our God-given purpose in a positive, greater way.

Your journey down the road to recovery can be very hard, both physically and mentally. You may feel like giving up at times because it hurts to deal with the pain, but do not give up! Hang on. It is well worth it to find healing in your life as God sets you free of all of the chains of your past that bind you and keep you weighed down in toxicity.

God desires healing for us all. Most importantly, God never leaves us; He walks each step of the way with us. And when we cannot take another step, He carries us.

As you will see in this book, God has carried me many times. He has never left me alone. When I look back I only see one set of footprints in the sand at times. He has carried me through the deep waters of my darkest days and set my feet upon dry, solid ground.

This book endeavors to describe how it feels to have these negative feelings. It also tells the good news about how we can overcome obstacles in our lives despite dark trials and tribulations. Christians are not exempt from hardship. Challenges, abuse and darkness may come our way, just the same as unbelievers experience—and sometimes even more! Our trials test our faith, hope and love for our God, and they also refine us like gold and build integrity and character while giving us strength in our Lord to successfully complete our appointed journey. The Bible says that believers should thank God for the fiery trials that come our way, for they are only to make us strong. Eventually we will begin to see and understand that we deserve to breathe the air that God has given us.

Beloved, think it not strange concerning the fiery trial which is to try you, as though some strange thing happened unto you. (1 Peter 4:12, KJV)

These have come so that your faith—of greater worth than gold, which perishes even though refined by fire—

may be proved genuine and may result in praise, glory and honor when Jesus Christ is revealed. (1 Peter 1:7, NIV)

To begin healing, we have to be in a safe place in our lives where we can receive the needed support and love as we walk through this very difficult task. Through the Lord and my counseling, I am learning about tools that help me achieve a healthy life. I still have a very long way to go, but the healing journey has begun!

Some people have these tools in their lives to help them respond and get through each of their trials. Others, like me, were never taught these valuable things. The awesome news is there is a wonderful God who sees our every tear and hears our every prayer. He feels our hurt, and He understands our broken hearts, and through Him we can find healing. I can say this with confidence in my heart because I have experienced the healing and presence of God. And I am still experiencing His healing power in my life today.

God is with you and wants you to call upon His name so He can be your help throughout your journey in life. "Call unto me, and I will answer thee, and show thee great and mighty things, which thou knowest not" (Jeremiah 33:3, KJV). There is no problem that is too great or too small for the Lord to handle. He wants to hear your heart's cry because He is there for you no matter what you have been through or what you are going through today. God heals the same today as Jesus did when He walked on this earth as the Son of God. "And Jesus went about all Galilee, teaching in their synagogues, and preaching the gospel of the kingdom, and healing all manner of sickness and all manner of disease among the people" (Matthew 4:23, KJV).

The Lord has a special plan for everyone's life and a journey for each one to travel. Whatever your journey is in life, God wants you to know that He loves you! And He is there for you, to travel with you, never to leave your side. All you need to do is ask Him to be a part of your life with a humble heart, and He will hear and answer you.

God is sad when bad things happen to His children, and He is there to help. You see, God has given each of us free choice, and some make very bad choices that end up hurting others. It states in Genesis 2:15–17,

And the LORD God took the man, and put him into the garden of Eden to dress it and to keep it. And the LORD God commanded the man, saying, Of every tree of the garden thou mayest freely eat: But of the tree of the knowledge of good and evil, thou shalt not eat of it: for in the day that thou eatest thereof thou shalt surely die. (KJV)

So, from the very beginning of time, God gave us responsibility and free choice. God could have easily physically prevented Adam from eating of the tree of knowledge of good and evil. Instead, He gave Adam a choice, knowing there was a possibility of him making a wrong choice. Free choice has been throughout the ages, and humans have made many wrong choices. These wrong choices may bring us pain, but if we choose to learn from them they can also help us to grow. This can help us make better choices in the future. We live with the consequences of our choices, which can teach us to become more responsible.

As you continue to read this book, please keep in mind that everyone may be in a different place in his or her journey. Hopefully some of the nuggets I have learned will help you in your life's journey. This in turn will assist you in finding the help you need to begin your healing.

It is my prayer that you will feel the loving presence of a caring God. He is my life, my strength, my guide, my best friend and the reason I can breathe the air He gives me each day with a very thankful heart. Singer-artist Michael W. Smith sings in one of my favorite songs, "This is the air I breathe, Your holy presence living in me…"[1] Jesus is the reason I am alive today; without Him I would have perished. I am sharing selected things from my past with you only so you can see that I understand your pain.

May God bless and keep you close to Him throughout your trials. May you find healing from the hurts of your past, and may you feel God's loving, caring presence within your soul. You are special, and you have a God-given purpose for your life. Seek and ye shall find.

Now, take a deep breath…
and
Breathe…

1.

Whose Air Is It Anyway?

And the LORD God formed man of the dust of the ground, and breathed into his nostrils the breath of life; and man became a living soul. (Genesis 2:7, KJV)

From the moment I entered into this earthly realm it did not feel like home to me. I have always struggled with where "my place on this earth" really is. I think this comes from the many dark, difficult trials and abuse that I have endured throughout my life. Through the many years of struggling to survive and searching to find a place where I could lay my head at night, fit in or belong, I have always had these haunting and convincing thoughts stuck in my mind: "I do not deserve the air that I breathe" and "I am breathing in someone else's air." I always felt I was not good enough to breathe the air on this earth; thus my existence was not validated. Why was I even here?

Many years later, I went to see my grandmother on my biological father's side. This was very hard for me to do, because there was great fear attached to this activity. She was the only one I had good memories of.

My grandmother was so thrilled to see me that she cried along with me for the whole visit. Grandmother had waited many years and prayed she would one day see me again. The time had finally come.

As I sat across the dining room table along with my older sister—by one year and a week—I listened to my grandmother unburden her heart about what really happened to me. It was very difficult to hear, and yet I felt as though I needed to know. Her story began with her coming to get me from the hospital when I was born so she could care for me. She told me that when she walked into the hospital room where I was, she gasped for air as she looked upon a baby who was very sick and premature. I looked near death. I cried when someone went to pick me up; I had already learned fear at this early age.

My grandmother took me home and nursed me back to health. This took quite a while to do, she told me, because I was so very afraid of many things. She shared with me that I would never make a sound and would cry into my sheets, afraid of what might happen if my voice was heard. My tears wet the sheets many times. I was very underweight and didn't trust anyone at all. Throughout my growing up years, I always felt this world was not really my home.

My grandmother told me that she was at peace now that she had the chance to tell me what had really happened. She was kind and gentle and, for the very short period of time I was with her, showed me love that others had not.

When I was twelve or thirteen months old, my parents took me back after persuading the court they would look after me and be responsible. My grandmother had no choice; she had to let me go with them. It was only months later when my grandmother once again came to my rescue. As it turned out, my mother was not capable at the time to care for me; in fact she was very abusive towards me. I was at the hospital with burns. At this young age, I had been placed in a laundromat's clothes dryer, and the dryer was turned on. It was only by the grace of God that I was found only minutes later, avoiding life-threatening burns and possibly death! A God-given angel who was in the bathroom of the laundromat came out and found me in a tumbling dryer. I was then taken to the hospital, and she reported what she had found.

As I look back on my life, I can see now why I continued to feel I was not good enough to breathe the air on this earth. Children who feel the love of their parents or caretakers from birth learn to feel validated and loved. This helps them to learn who they are in a healthy way. My feelings of rejection and not belonging led me to think that I was not deserving of the air I was breathing. My paternal grandmother cared for me as a babe in arms until my parents decided to prove to the courts again that they would be different this time. Many years later I thanked my grandmother with all my heart for what she had done for me. A few months after my visit, she passed away.

As I grew older and continued to live an unhealthy, dysfunctional life, I had to have determination to begin crawling the opposite way, away from the dysfunction I was surrounded with. This took the strength of God making a way for me. Through this process I am still journeying today. I still had this question in my heart: "Do I really even deserve to breathe the air that surrounds me?"

Breathing in air is very intricate and involves the whole body.[2] We inhale air through our mouths and noses, and it travels to our lungs. Breathing is controlled by the respiratory center located at the base of our brains. It's an involuntary action, meaning our bodies do not have to think about the breaths we take unless we are physically suffering with something that interferes with our breathing. We breathe all day and throughout the night, even when in an unconscious state. The oxygen that we breathe is carried through the bloodstream throughout our whole bodies, providing life to each and every muscle and cell. If there is too little oxygen in our blood, our bodies begin to breathe heavier and deeper to provide the needed oxygen. In normal, calm breathing a person usually breathes about fifteen times per minute. The work of breathing includes the diaphragm, the neck, the abdomen and the muscles between the ribs. Our nerves also play a big part in our breathing, but only if there's a healthy connection to our brain. The Lord even created a way for our bodies to exhale the toxins while getting rid of the carbon dioxide. Breathing is really a complex, God-given miracle that He has so graciously given unto us.

It's very evident that without air to breathe we would perish. It is the lifeline of existence for every human. Air is the very essence of life within us; it sustains us. From the moment we are born, we receive the gift of breathing the air God has placed on this earth; it is a gift given to us each day.

God has placed us all here for His purpose. It may take some time before we are aware of the purpose we are meant to achieve, but as we humbly seek the Lord, it will be revealed to us.

There are many different ways we can breathe. Breathing heavily with a rapid heartbeat can bring stress, which in turn can create problems in our physical bodies. Breathing slow, relaxed breaths can calm our physical and mental beings. The one proven fact about breathing in air is that it will support life if done right.

Breathing air in a healthy way helps to relax us, and thus it brings us peace and comfort at times. We can also experience times of panic or anxiety as we breathe heavily due to stressful situations. We all have a choice as to our breathing technique, unless we're in a situation where fear, abuse and trauma captivate us.

God gives each person air to sustain his or her life on this earth. There may be many who have felt the way I have. This is due to unhealthy thinking or wrongs that have been done unto us, making us feel invalidated as a person. If you are feeling this way, you may be experiencing little self-esteem and confidence in who you are. Negative things that occur can strip you of feeling like you deserve to breathe the air you have been given from God to sustain your life.

As I continue to grow through the help of God, counseling and those who love me, I can say now that the air I breathe today is a gift from God to me and that I deserve to breathe as God purposed on the day I was born. The air I breathe is His holy presence living in me.

Now, take a deep breath…
and
Breathe…

2.

Life's Journey

Jesus saith unto him, I am the way, the truth, and the life. (John 14:6, KJV)

Jesus is our life; we are all given a special journey. Our given journey specialized for each of us is to do the will of God, no matter the cost.

The moment we are born and take in that first God-given breath, we begin our journey. Each person has a story that is unique and has a place in this tapestry of life. You are needed, and you have a great part to play as you participate in weaving your threads that will help complete this beautiful tapestry of life. You may have been blessed to have a positive journey throughout your childhood, or your journey may have been a toxic one, which carries a lot of pain and stumbling blocks to get over. We are all called according to His purpose, that we may all do the will of God. "*And we know that in all things God works for the good of those who love him, who have been called according to his purpose*" (Romans 8:28, NIV).

Our journey in our life can be considered using a couple of analogies. I think it's much easier to understand the depth of reality when an analogy is used. Our first analogy involves garments of clothing. Life is like putting on and taking off garments you have in your closet. When you're young, you're clothed in garments that shape who you are to become. If you experience love, then the garment of love has been put on you. If you experience fear, then the garment of fear has been placed upon you. Maybe you wear the garment of low self-esteem, fear, mistrust, rejection and more. You can wear several different garments at the same time.

As we grow older and come to the age where we can choose for ourselves, we can choose to continue wearing the garments that have been placed upon us or to take off the unhealthy garments and heal so we can replace them with healthy garments. It is possible to heal; we just have to realize that our deep hurts are like peeling an onion one layer at a time. It may take longer for some, especially if they have deeper wounds to heal. It depends on how deep the layers are over the deep toxins buried within.

I look at growing up as putting on garments that make us who we are. Imagine a closet before you that has different garments hanging in it such as healthy self-esteem, low self-esteem, fear, trust, lack of trust, healthy self-confidence, lack of self-confidence, negative thoughts, positive thoughts and many more. When you were little, your caretakers usually dressed you. They hopefully put healthy garments on you, which let you experience healthy growth in many ways. This taught you the tools you needed to help you decipher healthy things and in turn helped you to make good choices in life as you matured.

On the other side of things, unhealthy garments may be placed on you instead. As you continued to wear these garments, unhealthy things were being formed within you as a small child, learning toxic life behaviors. You were being engrained in life skills from the garments you were wearing. They may be all you know in the moment.

Let's just say that I wore many toxic garments as a child growing up. For a very long time I've desired and longed for healing to have the strength to change the unhealthy garments I'm wearing to healthy ones. These garments of low self-esteem, lack of self-confidence, fear, lack of trust, rejection and negative thoughts, to name a few, are deeply rooted in who I am. As I grow older, the garments I've worn for many years are worn and feel comfortable, even though I really want to take them off. I start to see they are very toxic, and I need to get rid of them. But how can I do this? Have you ever felt like this?

You cannot do this alone. You need to seek help. My help has come from the Lord and His leading in my life and from those He has brought into my path who have so graciously been strength, encouragement and help to me. "*So that we may boldly say, The Lord is my helper, and I will not fear what man shall do unto me*" (Hebrews 13:6, KJV).

You see, now as an adult you have the free choice to go into your closet and change the garments you have on. Unfortunately, sometimes a certain garment is not so easy to take off, because it has become such a part of who you are. Before the toxic garment can be taken off, you have to find a new healthy garment and learn about the tools of that healthy garment. Then you can replace the toxic one with it. The only way you can do this is by the grace of God, who has opened this door of recovery so that you and God can begin the journey of healing.

Each layer or unhealthy garment represents our dark tumultuous experiences of our past hurts. Healing is painful but possible, with God's help! *"Heal me, O LORD, and I will be healed; save me and I will be saved, for you are the one I praise"* (Jeremiah 17:14, NIV).

We each came into this world with nothing and will leave with only what we have chosen to do for our Lord. May God help us all to search out the special calling He has chosen for each of us to complete with our Father in heaven's help.

My childhood, unfortunately, was not healthy, and I have had to climb over, under and around many stumbling blocks. If you have encountered this as well, then you are familiar with the hard work and pain we have to endure on the road in our journey of healing. I really don't like to speak about my childhood, but I will give a few highlights to help you understand that I know that pain.

I was born into a family who, for the most part, really never wanted me. So I went through physical and emotional abuse. The following is a poem I wrote that endeavors to express my broken heart but hopefully will bring healing as I learn to let go with the Lord's help.

SHE

Unwanted and rejected, she carried me
As she consistently strove to abort
The child that was growing inside of her,
All her efforts to succeed fell short.

Born into this world I came,
Full of bruises, beaten from within
Knowing and feeling FEAR, before birth,
I had already been engrained in.
Left in the hospital, abandoned, it's true
I was placed with my grandmother
It was what they chose to do.

As a babe in arms, I did not make a sound
I cried only silently,
Great FEAR did abound.
My tears silently wet the sheets,
I was scared, sick and frail.

It wasn't long before she came
And took me to her home in just one month,
She did something not many had known,
She placed me in a dryer,

The laundromat was just a couple quarters
The push of a button
For me to live was apparently God's will
Because…a woman came out of the bath-
room and rescued me!

She came in and out of my life,
Each time she brought great FEAR,
I would hide under and in everything
To escape her wicked will.

The beatings and abuse
In unspeakable ways they came
It was apparent that I was a mistake,
One she tried to erase.

She was my enemy, not my mom!
Those days are very dark and full of deep
pain,
Days I've tried to suppress, Rejected…
Never a home to call my own,
A wanderer, always running, unwanted
alone and scared, it has only been
By the grace of God
that my life was truly spared.

I was very afraid of the one who gave birth to me,
and this is one thing I'm learning to let go of. It will take
some time. It was only by the grace of God that I survived

all of the unhealthy things in my past. I compare this period of my life to walking and stumbling in a dark hole. I could not see in front of or behind me; it was just darkness and fear. I remember, the few times I was with my biological mother, the fear that never left me. It was like I had to walk on eggshells. She could become upset about the smallest things. I would be the one that had to face her wrath, which terrified me. I would hide behind doors, under beds, in closets—anywhere she could not find me. As mentioned before, I had great fear instilled in me! I was not allowed to wrinkle my dress, so I could not sit down; I had to stand most of the time. I was supposed to keep busy with household tasks at all times. If she walked by and saw I wasn't busy or productive cleaning, I would receive her wrath. I had learned very quickly not to relax, read a book or do things most children my age did. This has spilled over into my life today; I still feel guilt if I try to relax! I am trying hard to work on this.

I learned to use my heightened senses well when still very young. I could sense when she came home and had been drinking. It could go either way; she could be very abusive or unusually nice. It was usually the former. She became so very frightening to me when under the influence. One day she became so mad that she threw a pair of scissors at me. The point just barely missed my head; I was just grazed by them. They did, however, go all the way through the bathroom door!

These are just a few things I have chosen to share, through the grace of God, to show you that I understand the deep trials others have gone through experiencing fear of and rejection by their caretakers. I would dream of having a home and family where I could grow up without any fear.

I have grown to a place where I have forgiven the things I went through with my mother. It was anything but healthy. I cannot forget the pain and I still wear the scars, but I do sincerely forgive her.

I was in and out of foster homes for most of my childhood. I was tossed to and fro. In fact, I never had a family set a good foundation for me so I could learn the healthy things loving families instill in their children. I think back to my younger years, and they were very hard, vague, and deeply toxic. Most of my days were filled with fear and rejection while I constantly had to learn survival techniques. Rejection has seized me many times in my life. There are a lot of holes in my memories, because I've blocked them out due to posttraumatic stress, which I have suffered all my life. I have learned that this was manifested from the impact of the physical and emotional abuse of my childhood.

I have chosen to go through counseling with the help of God, to help me heal from the toxic wounds of my past. This is and has been one of the hardest things in my journey. I had to choose to travel down the road of recovery. None of us really wants to go back and face past darkness, such as abuse from others, poor choices made for us, and many other toxic things that have molded us into who we are today.

I'm finally at the place where I can safely work on the toxicity of my past. I thank God for this. I thank God for my wonderful, kind and loving husband, who has been and is always by my side through it all. He is strength for me, sent from heaven above. Thank You, Father in Heaven!

The good news is that there is healing from our toxic past! It all begins with the help and guidance of our wonderful Lord. "*O LORD my God, I called to you for help and you healed me*" (Psalm 30:2, NIV).

Once you begin on the road to healing, it will be hard, and there may be days when you want to run and hide or stay in bed and pull the covers up over your head. I encourage you to cling to the Lord, and He will give you the strength you need to heal the wounds, no matter how deep they are and no matter how long it takes! This healing cannot be rushed. In fact, throughout your healing there will be many days when you can only take baby steps.

If you experience triggers from your past, as I have and still do, you may feel like you are going backwards. Keep pressing on! You cannot rush your healing process. Sometimes the toxic past has to be broken down into small bits in order to process and remove each and every part of your poisonous toxins. God will help you fill where the toxins once were with His love and grace as you heal throughout your journey. "*Nevertheless, I will bring health and healing to it; I will heal my people and will let them enjoy abundant peace and security*" (Jeremiah 33:6, NIV).

When growing up, I never went to one school for a whole year. I was the focus of much physical, emotional and psychological abuse from many different people in my life. A lot of toxic abuse happened within my biological family, as well from strangers and friends. My birth parents didn't take responsibility for looking after and caring for me, their biological child, in a loving way. I was not validated or valued at all; instead I was shown how much of a mistake I was. My biological family had many problems, which in turn were taken out on the children. The caregivers were focused on themselves, which gave me no security or sense of belonging. I, in turn, had to learn to parent myself, which was a very hard thing to do and really beyond what a small child should have to do.

My maternal step-grandfather abused me many times in my young life. He made me partake of many abusive things, and I was consistently told it was for my good and that every young girl needed to learn these things to prepare her for her future. He passed away many years back, but before his passing I went to their home, with the support of my wonderful husband, which was one of the hardest and scariest things I have ever done! Once there I felt the presence of our Lord with me. I knelt on the living room floor, looking into his eyes, and I forgave him for what he had repeatedly done to me when I had lived in their home. He never looked up at me, and he denied his abusive behavior towards me, even on this very hard day as I forgave him. I knew going into his house that there was no guarantee that I would be welcomed, and I was not.

A lot had happened to me from my relatives that brought much pain in my life. I felt I needed to forgive so a heavy weight could be lifted off of my shoulders, and the Lord heard my heart's cry and lifted that burden I had carried for so long, which I have learned now was not mine to carry at all.

An uncle (my maternal grandmother's son) also abused me, and I was very afraid of him as well. One of my questions I have grown up with is "How is it that no one knew the horrible incest and abuse that was going on right under their noses, in their houses?" I tried to talk about it with them, but fear quickly seized me due to their negative reactions. I knew I shouldn't do that. I was told that if anyone outside of the family knew, I would be called a liar to my face. Besides, they told me many times that no one would believe me, because I was just a child!

There is good news...

God can help you through the tangled web of an unhealthy childhood like mine. It won't be easy; it takes a lot of time, effort, support and faith. It is one of the hardest things you will ever decide to do. You cannot do it alone! You need to give all you are over to God and lean on His strength, guidance and wisdom, moment by moment instead of day by day. He will not let you down.

Now, take a deep breath...
and
Breathe...

$3.$

To Live or Not to Live, That Is the Question

---

*O*f course the answer to this question is: Choose life! Even when there seems to be no life purpose and the road seems so dark you cannot find your way!

I have experienced depression. As I have struggled at times with the dark illness, I ask myself, "Why is my desire gone to do even the most simplest tasks each day, and how long will this continue?" There are days when I dread getting out of bed. In fact, depression has been prevalent at times throughout my life, and much more so when I was experiencing deep, difficult trials of rejection, abuse and sickness. The more I heal from the wounds of my past, the less the depression seems to be.

On the other side of things, when God has picked me up and brought me out of the depths of despair, I am a very ambitious, motivated person with God's help. Otherwise I wouldn't still be breathing the air I breathe to this day. God gets the glory for bringing me from depression to living with purpose. I know it was God who carried me when life tried to pull me down into the deep, dark hole of depression. I have worked, with God, my way through raising seven children, completing my teaching degree at university later in life, teaching grades 11 and 12, and being here for my family and the people God has brought my way. I have a great love for others, especially the lonely and hurting.

It was engrained in me throughout my childhood that I was worthless and would never amount to anything. I felt that I needed to strive to prove the naysayers wrong. The Lord walked with me through the halls of university and helped me each step of the way. God walked across the graduation stage together with my wonderful husband and me. We graduated university together. Thank you, Lord, for helping me complete my teaching degree, because there were days when I really thought I would not make it!

Unfortunately, life sometimes has a way of beating us down physically, emotionally and spiritually. When I reached a certain point in my teaching career, I became ill and unfortunately had to go on sick leave. Now I feel in my heart that the Lord has used this difficult time to start me dealing with my past that has been deeply locked away and learning tools I can use to experience a healthier life. It's very hard for me, but I'm determined to learn new tools and to unlock and remove the pains of my past.

In doing so, I have experienced depression once again. It's like a black cloud that hangs over you everywhere you go. It's almost like your physical body is waving a white surrender flag to represent your weariness in your journey. Anyone who has suffered with depression—and the numbers are very high—cannot just get up one morning and be completely over it! It's a long and hard journey to healing. And God is the only one who can pick us up and set us on our feet in the right direction, helping us climb out of that dark pit that depression brings to our souls.

So the question "To live or not to live" is a very important one. God wants us to live and glorify His name, but sometimes our negative self-talk tells us that it's time to quit. We feel we have no more strength to go on. Have you ever felt this way? I have, many times over.

The truthful answer to the question presented is to "Live!" God will never leave us or forsake us. He will help us live each day in Him. There will be very difficult days ahead, but if we allow Him, Jesus will be our protector and guide. *"So then, just as you received Christ Jesus as Lord, continue to live your lives in him, rooted and built up in him"* (Colossians 2:6–7, TNIV).

This is the reason we were born, so that we can be ambassadors of His will. We can't really do this if we are deep in depression and suffering from the pains of the past. It can seize our every thought, move and desire to go on. It also has a great negative effect on our physical bodies, as it has on mine.

There are those that do not and cannot really understand depression, especially if they have never experienced it for themselves—and I personally would not want them to experience it. But it would be good for others to strive to research depression and the huge grip it can have on its prey. Many things can cause depression, everything from low physical health to emotional trauma. Depression is a real illness and is the aftermath of things our bodies cannot handle on their own. It's a result from struggling through many things that are emotional and physical.

Depression is anger turned inward, inflicted upon yourself. In the Bible, Job was a man of God, and yet he suffered tremendously. He was being tested to see how his love and loyalty would stand for his Lord. There was even a time when he wanted to die because he didn't understand why God was allowing these horrible trials to be brought upon him.

Job was looked upon as a man of integrity, one who walked in the ways of our Lord both day and night, helping those who suffered and feeding the hungry, while his door was always open for those who needed counsel.

"But now they mock me" (Job 30:1, NIV). When all seemed too much for Job, through his pain and suffering he spoke unto our Lord. *"Even today my complaint is bitter; his hand is heavy in spite of my groaning"* (Job 23:2 NIV). *"I put on righteousness as my clothing; justice was my robe and my turban"* (Job 29:14 NIV).

Do you ever feel others are condemning or judging you due to their lack of understanding in the trials you go through? Job used healthy anger to express his feelings about what his friends were accusing him of as well as his lack of understanding of why these trials had come his way.

I have been through many trials in my journey, and I have never understood completely why they occurred. I eventually came to the place where I needed to stop trying to understand why everything happened and just put my trust and faith in our Lord.

Faith does not only believe God can; it knows He will! I have been in and out of the hospital more times than I can count. For example, in 1981 I suffered with kidney stones, which led to major surgery, and I was in the hospital for eight weeks. I had three small children at home; my baby was only six weeks old. This was so very difficult for me; I was so sick and worried about my family during this trial.

In 1989, I contracted spinal meningitis and encephalitis simultaneously. I was hospitalized for ten weeks. I went into a coma and was not expected to live. The doctors said if for some small reason I did survive these illnesses, I would be institutionalized and unable to function on my own each day for the rest of my life. All of the nerve endings along my spinal cord were infected, and as a result I was unable to walk or feel anything from the waist down. My body went into involuntary spasms. The doctors had to brace me to the hospital bed so I wouldn't fall off during the spasms. The encephalitis created a buildup of fluid in the lining of my brain, making it impossible for me to lift my head even a small fraction of an inch off of my pillow. I drifted in and out of consciousness and could at times hear people talking, crying and stating the grim fact that I would never pull through.

I did awaken from the coma, to find out how badly my body had been affected. The only way I can speak of this dark time in my life today is that there were many praying for me all over the world. God touched me and healed me! Even though I was so very thankful for the healing, it was still a challenge for me, because I had to learn to walk all over again and slowly learn how to hold my head up. Eventually the migraine headaches became fewer and fewer. Today I have very few side effects from the toxic illness that ravaged my body. All the glory goes to my Heavenly Father, who touched me and healed me.

It took over two years to get my health back to where I could look after my family on my own. In fact, doctors I see even today still shake their heads and tell me I shouldn't have survived. I thank you, Lord, for giving me life and air to breathe once again.

This dark illness also brought deep depression into my life. Years later, I began taking a counseling class on depression. The group leaders asked the class to draw a picture of what depression looked and felt like. I drew a huge dark cloud over me as I was stuck in a dark, dark hole. I drew some lightning bolts all around the hole. There seemed to be no way out at all.

When the group members showed and talked about their drawings, I was shocked. There were similarities in all of our pictures. The dark cloud, dark hole, monsters, and thunderbolts were all included. We each knew nothing of what the others were drawing!

We then talked about depression, summing it up as feeling like you're falling off a cliff into a dark endless hole. Many feel hopeless and out of control. We were taught that the dark cloud of depression could be pushed aside as we used the healthy tools that we learned about. This is very, very hard to do, but as we grow in knowledge and understanding of our depression it can eventually be done, especially with the help of our Lord!

You need to know that if you are suffering from depression, you are *not* alone! The studies have shown that more than 4 percent of adults are experiencing depression at any given time. And nearly 15 percent of adults will be depressed at some time in their lives! If you are experiencing or have experienced depression, it is not a sign of weakness. It happens in *all* walks of life. It also does *not* mean that you may have a "weak personality" or any "character flaws."

Depression is more than just a low mood. It can certainly have a big effect on a person's thoughts, feelings, physical functioning and whole being. There are many different types of depression. One who suffers with depression may have one or more of the following symptoms: Sadness, despair throughout the day, an inability to enjoy activities that you may normally get pleasure from, feeling unusually anxious and irritated or angry. You may also feel worthlessness, shame or guilt. Fatigue may be present and significant weight loss or weight gain. It may be very hard to sleep at night, or you may wake early and be unable to fall back asleep. Sometimes depression can bring hypersomnia, which is sleeping much more than usual. These are just a few of the symptoms related to depression.

The definition of depression consists of prolonged awareness of lowered mood associated with a loss of enjoyment in usually pleasurable circumstances and feelings. One may feel loss of enjoyment with feelings of hopelessness. It is possible one also may feel lack of initiative, difficulty in making decisions, irritability or anger.

The good news is that depression can be overcome in a lot of cases! Sometimes it will take a long time, so do not become discouraged. Those with depression need to hear positive affirmations each day to help them pull out of the dark, depressing hole they find themselves in. When I experience depression, I feel that my body is telling me that it has had enough and it needs to heal from the trauma I have gone through.

Depression is a very intricate illness and is such a huge struggle for many who are experiencing it. As mentioned earlier, it's like your body has gone on strike and needs healing to catch up to the everyday activities that life brings us. While suffering from depression, we lose the desire to even do the everyday things that have to be done in life.

Do not give up, even when you feel like it! Do not beat yourself up over the low mood you are feeling. There is help. Call out to Jesus. Call a friend or crisis line, and remember, God is always there for you!

Now, take a deep breath…
and
Breathe…

4.

Do Our Choices Bring Consequences?

---

*But if you refuse to serve the LORD, then choose today
whom you will serve. Would you prefer the gods your
ancestors served beyond the Euphrates? Or will it be the
gods of the Amorites in whose land you now live? But as
for me and my house, we will serve the LORD.*
(Joshua 24:15, NLT)

o our choices bring consequences? The answer is "Yes." Every human on this earth has the right to make his or her own choices. Once they reach the age of adulthood they are given a gift from God, to make their own life choices.

As a child, the choices are the responsibility of the parents or caregivers. At this time of life, the parents or caregivers gently lead and teach the child right from wrong and the positive and negatives of how to make choices. And I am sure the Lord is hoping and waiting for each to take ownership and make the best choices they can for the children who are placed under their care. Unfortunately, there are many young ones who do not get a healthy upbringing because of the poor choices that their caregivers make. If you have been raised in a loving, caring home, then take a moment to thank our Father in heaven. It makes His heart glad! Give your loving parents a hug!

For children like me who had to struggle through the darkness and pain of poor decisions made by their toxic caregivers, God shed many tears as He looked upon our journeys. "*Streams of tears flow from my eyes, for your law is not obeyed*" (Psalm 119:136, NIV).

You may be wondering why God would allow such pain to come into your life as a child. You could not change your circumstances. Why would God abandon you and let you go through such horrific pain and trials? Is there really a God?

Yes, there really is a God, and He cares for you! He never leaves you, even through your darkest pain. Remember, God gave people a gift of free choice, and it does not make Him happy to see His little ones suffer from the bad choices people make.

When we make a bad choice it doesn't affect only us. Our choices have a ripple effect and touch other lives. It's like throwing a stone into the water; there are always ripples. Think of those ripples as people who are affected by the choices we make. There are consequences that occur from our choices. If we make good choices, then we will reap good consequences. If we make poor choices, then we will reap hard consequences. So consequences can be either good or bad, depending on the choices we make, but try to understand that there will be a consequence either way!

We've all made poor choices, because we are mere human. It doesn't mean we're failures. Hopefully we can look back and learn good lessons from our not so good choices.

My husband and I have made a joint decision to not talk about difficult things after 7:00 p.m. if it can be helped. I have found that if we don't adhere to this, it causes lack of sleep and worry. If a choice has to be made, it's better to look at the situation when we're rested and at our best. Striving to set goals that will lessen anxiety can help everyone.

God desires us to make good choices that will please Him and cause our life to reap good things. The Bible says that good choices are better than silver and His knowledge is better than the finest gold: "*Choose my instruction instead of silver, knowledge rather than choice gold*" (Proverbs 8:10, NIV). Sometimes making a choice is easier when we've had time to think and pray about it.

We instill in our children at a very young age how to make good choices in hopes they will follow what they have learned by making good choices. If you have tried with all your might to teach your children and they choose to make poor choices, then don't take on the guilt of their choices; it is not yours to carry. The apostle Paul put it another way when he wrote, "*Do not be deceived, God is not mocked; for whatever a man sows, that he will also reap*" (Galatians 6:7, NKJV).

Again, the choices we make today will affect others around us as well. As we walk through our journey in life, just remember that our choices are like sowing seeds, so what a man sows, he will reap. Paul's words form a stark reminder to us that our choices have consequences—and that includes how we choose to treat others. When we choose to hate, that hate can return to us in the form of consequences that we can never fully prepare for. We can find ourselves alienated from others, angry with ourselves, and hamstrung in our ability to serve Christ effectively. Instead, let's choose to "*not grow weary while doing good, for in due season we shall reap…As we have opportunity, let us do good to all*" (Galatians 6:9–10, NKJV). The seeds we sow today determine the kind of fruit we'll reap tomorrow.

> Sowing seeds of greed and hatred
> Reaps corruption, loss, and pain;
> But if we sow love and kindness,
> We will reap eternal gain.—Sper[3]

Do you know your values? Knowing your values will help you make better choices. It will also help you to align your choices with your values. Knowing your values will also help you to find people, places and things that will be compatible with you, and this will bring more meaning into your life. It is best to choose healthy things in your life while looking to the Lord to help remove the toxins from your past. Making the right choices will bring much peace and joy into your life as you allow our heavenly Father to be your help and to guide through your journey here.

Now, take a deep breath...
and
Breathe...

5.

Shame versus Guilt

Those who look to him are radiant; their faces are never covered with shame. (Psalm 34:5, NIV)

Shame and guilt are different things. Guilt can actually be a constructive emotion. Healthy guilt helps us to see when we have done something wrong; therefore it can be an asset if used in the right way.

When you feel guilt it should help you to recognize that something you have done may have been wrong, causing another person pain. Guilt is feeling sorry for something you did wrong and can lead you to making amends.

Shame, on the other hand, is a harmful emotion. It affects your self-esteem in a negative way. It gives you the feeling of being a bad person. Instead of feeling sorry for the person you've harmed or the one who has harmed you, you feel sorry for who you are.

The same action can make one person feel shame and another person feel guilt. Healthy guilt usually comes with both feelings of remorse and regret. The guilty person is usually very sorry for his or her actions and wants to make things right with the one hurt. Those who experience guilt will usually strive not to repeat the same actions in the future.

Shame can also cause feelings of repentance and at times pain and humiliation. Abusers and perpetrators usually use shame upon us. They use shame to make the victims feel they are not good enough or worthy to seek help on the outside.

Clearly stated, guilt is at work when you feel bad about what you have done, and shame is at work when you feel bad about who you are as a person. Shame frustrates and humiliates us, where healthy guilt helps us see when we've done something wrong. Guilt can actually keep a person on a good path. For instance, shame says there's something wrong with me where healthy guilt tells me I've done something wrong and my conscience will want me to make right what I've done wrong.

We must not wear the garment of shame from abuse others have inflicted upon us. "*Let the words of my mouth, and the meditation of my heart, be acceptable in thy sight, O LORD, my strength, and my redeemer*" (Psalm 19:14, KJV).

The first time I had an "Aha" moment concerning shame and guilt was when we were going over the topic "Shame vs. Guilt" in our counseling class. It hit me like a ton of bricks and really helped me to see things from a different perspective. All these many years, I'd been blaming myself for the offenses that happened to me as a child. I'd been using negative thinking to reinforce that guilt and shame. The real feeling I have been carrying and living through had been mostly shame. For the first time I recognized a huge difference! I don't do well with rejection because I have suffered too much of it throughout my life. I've been abandoned many times by my biological mother and father, different chosen caretakers, family and acquaintances.

Do not let the perpetrator win! You need to only own what is yours. Do not carry the guilt and shame of the perpetrator. When we carry the blame—the guilt and shame and poison of the abuse, the perpetrator is free, and the victim is paying the price for what the offender has chosen to do.

Can you imagine giving up the self-destructive, self-defeating, negative and poisonous thinking, refusing to carry it anymore? This will slowly happen as you begin to heal. By doing this, you are freeing yourself from the perpetrator!

Judgment is a huge, complex activity that leaves victims depleted of strength, depending on the severity of the judgment they have received from others. Judgment of me began at an early age, and I in turn learned to treat myself the same harsh way, often harsher than those judging me, because it did not come alone. It carried with it shame, guilt and low self-confidence, so this is how I learned to perceive myself. "*For in the same way you judge others, you will be judged, and with the measure you use, it will be measured to you*" (Matthew 7:2, NIV). When

I gave up self-judgment and honored myself as a survivor from my childhood, it was very foreign to me until I had worn it for a while. I was constantly hard on myself and knew no other way. I have been seeking the Lord for direction and strength as I travel down the road learning to like myself. I'm tired of always putting myself down, and I'm ready to stop carrying the guilt and shame others have put upon me.

Have you ever felt this way? There is healing for the things we have gone through, and God is definitely ready to hear our cry so He can help us learn and heal from our abusive past. Again, it will take a different amount of time for each one, depending on the depth of our abuse and our desire to heal.

We should be very careful when it comes to the word *judgment*. God is our only honest and fair judge. *"By myself I can do nothing; I judge only as I hear, and my judgment is just, for I seek not to please myself but him who sent me"* (John 5:30, NIV). Jesus has been given the right to fairly judge us as God our Father has bestowed this upon Him. We must be very careful with one another; Christ can see our hearts and knows the truth of both sides. That is why He is a fair and just judge.

Growing up, I longed to be part of a loving family. While most children were experiencing normal childhood things, I dreamed about, wanted and longed for a family that I could love and that would love me back. I was tired of having to find my next meal and a place to lay my head at night, tired of trying to keep myself safe and not frightened. The world to me was a scary place. It seemed to me that someone always wanted something immoral from me! Unfortunately, going through tremendous abuse from others, I lost a very important ability. I felt I could trust no one. It has always been very hard for me to trust others. I am working hard on learning to do this.

I have never felt good enough for anyone or anything. I only felt like I was a good person if others liked and accepted me. I went out of my way to have those in my life care for and like me. It was as if I really needed their approval and acceptance to move on in my journey. I am talking about going to the ends of the earth to receive their love and acceptance! And when all of my ceaseless striving—trying to change something that I cannot change, trying so hard to have others like and love me—failed, I was crushed and depressed and once again started feeling guilt and shame.

Throughout my life, since I was a small infant, I have been a recipient of rejection. Hardly ever being picked up or loved as a baby and child, I lost all confidence in others and my worth. Negative thoughts kept flooding in, which kept me down in the pit of guilt and shame. I really never knew how to like myself. I'm sure it stems from the fact that as a small child I was never taught to value myself. No one ever valued me. I saw myself as nothing! In fact, every time I would have a good thought about myself, either great or small, I would quickly dismiss it, and I would feel guilt or shame for even thinking about or doing something for myself. I've learned that those who have been traumatically abused often do not know how to practice self-care. I was never taught the tools needed to heal before now. I had a way of carrying everyone else's problems along with my own, when the truth was that I was falling apart myself. Once again, I really never knew how to like myself. I saw myself as nothing and felt the guilt and shame instead.

The good news is that there is a way to find healing! *"He heals the brokenhearted And binds up their wounds"* (Psalm 147:3, NKJV). It doesn't matter how old you are when you begin the road to recovery. It's always possible with God's help and by forging through with the right help and counseling God leads you to. You can learn the right tools needed to live in a healthy environment. It may be scary for some; it has been for me, like a totally different garment. When you try it on, it feels very foreign if you have never worn it or learned the tools needed to wear it. But you can learn the right tools needed to live in a healthy environment. This will be one of the hardest things you will ever work on. It is well worth it, because you are learning to forge a new healthy pathway you can walk on!

Don't get me wrong, caring and giving to others in need is a very good thing. If God has called you to minister to others in some capacity of giving, then this is your God-given purpose in life. If your feelings about yourself are toxic, then your priorities are not in the right order. As one of many who have gone through dark trials out of their control, I'm learning that there is still healing available. It is *never* too late to begin our journey toward healing.

Now, take a deep breath…
and
Breathe…

6.

"Anger"…Just One Letter Away from "Danger!"

"In your anger do not sin": Do not let the sun go down while you are still angry. (Ephesians 4:26, NIV)

What is anger? It's a healthy tool if used in the right way toward healing the hurts we carry from others. It's a normal emotion, an automatic inner response when we feel frustrated, hurt, afraid, or devalued. We only feel anger when something we value is being threatened. The angrier we are, the deeper we care. Anger is a healthy emotion; it's how we express the anger that can make it unhealthy.

Sometimes, I get as far away from anger as I can! I have learned that "anger" is just one step away from "danger." I am learning how to be angry in a healthy way, which is good. It's very hard, because I find it hard to feel or express anger. I set a goal for myself to learn how to express anger in a healthy way.

Feeling anger is a healthy part of healing from the hurts of our past if looked at with the right perspective. Healthy anger helps to keep us on the right path in life. Otherwise God would not have given us anger along with all our other emotions. We just have to learn to use it in a healthy way that helps us grow and heal. Unexpressed anger, if left smoldering too long, brings us anxiety and other physical problems. It is not healthy to block up our anger; we must learn how to bring it out in a healthy way.

"For his anger lasts only a moment, but his favor lasts a lifetime; Weeping may remain for a night, but rejoicing comes in the morning" (Psalm 30:5, TNIV). We see in this verse that God does get angry, but He does not hold on to His anger. He uses anger to help deal with the situation at hand in a healthy way and then quickly dismisses it so healing may come in its time. We also see that, even though He displays His anger, rejoicing will come in the morning and that His favor toward us last a lifetime!

Anger and aggression are totally different. Anger is an emotion while aggression refers to a set of behavior traits directed at destroying objects and injuring or punishing people. Aggression is always destructive.

It's imperative that we accept responsibility for our own anger and how we handle it. Showing our anger through negative behavior, like destroying things and hurting others, is unhealthy. If we use our anger effectively with a good attitude to help resolve a problem, it can assist us in dealing with sources of hurt and pain. *"But you, O Lord, are a compassionate and gracious God, Slow to anger, abounding in love and faithfulness"* (Psalm 86:15, NIV).

Learning to use our anger in constructive ways can help resolve issues that arise in our lives. It's never easy, because sometimes our first instinct is revenge against the one who hurt us and caused us pain. We can look at anger as an iceberg; the tip of the iceberg sticking out above the water is the anger others see. The part that lies underneath the water is all of our unmet needs, hurts and feelings no one sees. The more we hide our hurts, negative feelings, and abuse, the more unhealthiness is created within us. If we're hanging on to the anger, it's really hurting us. We're carrying a load that's too big for us and possibly not even ours to carry! Remember, our attitude and feelings give us initiative for our behavior.

So there are two types of anger, healthy anger and harmful anger. How do we know the difference? *Healthy anger* is expressed with caring or respect and a desire to restore a relationship. When we're expressing healthy anger we attack the problem, not the person. *Harmful anger* is expressed out of a desire to seek revenge and attack or hurt the person without any concern for restoring the relationship or resolving the problem. When we use anger as a harmful emotion, it can have a very negative impact on the person we're directing it towards.

Growing up, I was never around anyone who showed anger in a healthy way. I witnessed only harmful anger, and as I became older it created many unhealthy emotions—fear, lack of trust, and withdrawal. I have always had a problem with anger. It scares me, probably because of all the things I have endured from my past. I never even knew there was such an emotion as healthy anger. I always thought it was bad and related very closely with danger. Anger was a frightening thing, so I suppressed my anger as quickly as I could when I felt it emerge. Fear had built up within me, and I determined not to entertain the thought of anger at all. I didn't recognize that I was angry, and I turned it within. I realize that I have been angry for many years, inflicting this emotion in an unhealthy way by directing it towards my inner self, not even understanding I was angry about my past! I absorbed it into my inner self through constant negative self-talk, self-hatred, and treating myself badly. That was the safest way to express the emotion that I was so very afraid of. After all, it was normal for me to practice self-defeating behavior through low self-esteem, negative talk, and no self-care, hating myself day after day. And I never knew this is what I was doing until I learned healthy tools from counseling. I refused to believe I was even entertaining this scary emotion, but anger was there within me whether I wanted to own it or not.

God wants us to be good to ourselves because He made us and we are special in His eyes. As we heal, learning how to incorporate these healthy tools, we will change our lives for the better; we will learn to like ourselves and treat ourselves in a good and healthy way, as God intends.

Too many people in my life demonstrated harmful anger toward me instead of healthy anger. As I progress through very good counseling, I'm amazed at the things I was robbed of knowing as a child. I never learned there was even a difference in anger until recently! I was never allowed to express anger at all. I was taught that anger was dangerous—it's just one letter away from danger! So I kept my feelings inside, not knowing how to deal with them. By doing this I have been harming myself. When I found out about healthy anger and harmful anger, I felt sad that others never took the time to teach me important life skills that we each have a right to know and experience.

I believe it's never too late to learn healthy ways in which to live. I know the Lord was with me as I endeavored to raise my children because I would continuously seek Him for wisdom and guidance. I didn't have the experience of growing up in a healthy, functioning home to look back upon for guidance. Every home may have some dysfunction in one way or another, but a solid grounding in life begins as a small child in a caring home where you are valued as an individual. I always told my children, and still do, that I love them. I never heard those words while growing up, and I want all of my children to know without a doubt how much I love them.

If you haven't had the opportunity to be a part of a healthy home, it's not too late to learn. It's very difficult to do, but if the determination and desire is within you, then with God's help and guidance, good counseling and a support group, it is possible. The Lord has never let me down, for which I am very thankful.

Were you denied the right to feelings of anger? Maybe it's something you've never been taught. You've carried blame for what happened to you with the poison of guilt, shame, negative thinking, poor self-esteem, and destructive living. If you can use your anger in an effective way, it can help you deal with sources of pain in your life. Everyone has a right to feel the emotion of healthy anger and appropriately express that anger.

Healthy anger can be looked at as a gauge. It's an emotion that gives a check within if we need to make a change. It tells us we have been violated or hurt inside. When we get this check within, we can choose to stop and look at the situation, and using the right attitude of healthy anger, we can endeavor to resolve our problems in a healthy way. When Jesus walked the earth He displayed healthy anger to demonstrate the right thing to do. *"The LORD is compassionate and gracious, slow to anger, abounding in love"* (Psalm 103:8, NIV).

Anger, if used effectively, will help you resolve differences in constructive ways while getting closer to others. Were your feelings of anger growing up valued? Were you taught the difference between healthy and harmful anger? How do you react when you're angry? Do you recognize it as anger? Some of the symptoms many feel when angry are tense muscles, a chill or sweating, deeper and faster or light and slow breathing, and headaches. Do you get mean and destructive and blame others, or do you take ownership and work it out in a healthy way? Do you try to please others to avoid the conflict even though you are not at fault? Some may laugh or become sarcastic, and other people become quiet and withdrawn. Some may struggle with eating and sleeping too little or too much.

Learning how to deal with anger in a healthy way is a very important thing you can do for yourself and your loved ones. If you've never been taught, it's not too late to learn. It's like someone has lifted a ton off of your shoulders when you learn how to express anger in a healthy way. If you've grown up in fear of someone else's anger towards you, you do have a choice as an adult to learn the right way. It will change your life and help you to remove the fear you've learned! Remember, you have the free choice to make your own decisions as an adult whom God loves and values.

Keeping a journal of your feelings may help you to express your anger and prepare you to deal with your problems. I have always tried to keep a journal about my feelings, though it has been very difficult at times. Taking a time-out or cooling off period is another way of providing an opportunity to think things through before you approach the emotion of anger.

It's my prayer that you will look to God and choose to learn healthy ways to express your anger. Your life will be changed!

Now, take a deep breath...
and
Breathe...

7.

Self-Worth and Self-Esteem

———————

hat is self-worth? It's having a sense of one's own value or worth as a person and a healthy self-confidence. It means you place healthy value on who you are. It is when you feel equivalent to others and that you are unique and worthy of breathing the air that is given to you in this world. When you have self-worth, you can realize and rejoice that you are a valuable person.

What is self-esteem? It's individually ascribed value. It's an overall emotional evaluation. Do you suffer from low self-esteem? Do you believe, like I have for many years, that we must earn other people's love and approval by the good we strive to do? This is not true! We have the right to be loved and valued for who we really are.

As a child, I was shown that I had little to no value. In fact, there was so much negativity brought my way that I grew up without self-esteem. Survival was the focus of my life. I learned at a very young age to retreat within myself because it was safer. If I could have made myself invisible, I would have. Believe me, I tried both hiding and withdrawing. I quickly became a quiet, withdrawn child who lacked self-confidence, self-esteem and self-worth. I learned unhealthy things like fear, lack of trust, and how to survive on my own. I didn't think others liked me unless I did things to earn their love and acceptance. I constantly worked at making others like me; this is how I felt I was valued as a person. I experienced so much rejection that I was afraid to get close to others as I grew up. This was from rejection, abuse and negativity in my life. If you have felt this way, then I understand your struggles, and so does God. Our brokenness can actually give us opportunities for growth and self-acceptance.

What is dignity? It's "the quality of being worthy of esteem or respect";[4] the sense of one's own value or worth as a person; self-esteem; self-respect.

The question is, Do we have self-worth? A healthy self-worth is instilled in us as children. How do we measure our self-worth? Our true value is how God estimates our worth. Our peers, family and friends may evaluate and judge us according to how we present ourselves and live our lives, but God cares for and loves us because we belong to Him.

God is aware of everything that happens to us in our lives. *"The very hairs of your head are all numbered. Fear ye not therefore, ye are of more value than many sparrows"* (Matthew 10:30–31, KJV). If He loves the sparrows with such great love, then think of the great love He has for you. He sent His Son to die on the cross for us! God places great value upon you and me. We don't need to fear the arrows that fly by day or night; our loving God is here for us, every step through our journey here on this earth. When the fiery trials come, we are not alone! Our self-worth is hidden in Christ, our Savior. *"I love those who love me, and those who seek me find me"* (Proverbs 8:17, NIV).

When I was in my teens, the Lord gave me a vision that is still as vivid today as the day it happened. I was standing on the bank of a great, deep, rushing river. I could see the other side; it looked so far away, unattainable, and that's where I knew I should be. I felt God calling me to cross over to the other side of the river and begin my journey with Him. I was always running from many offenders, and I had a deep longing to be on the other side. I didn't know how to swim, so I was very afraid. I saw myself step into the raging water, and before I knew it, I was being tossed to and fro. Then I actually felt the arms of the Lord lift me up out of my despair and carry me to the other side! I have never looked back.

There have been many times when I've felt very little self-worth. I've felt like I don't measure up, and that's why I sometimes feel I am breathing someone else's air. My negative thinking tells me every day that I am worthless; therefore I do not claim the air I breathe as mine. This type of thinking can destroy self-worth and create depression that is very toxic.

We live in a world where many struggle and many want to give up. Everyone is here for a reason, and that is to love and serve our Heavenly Father each day of our lives. *"But I trust in your unfailing love; my heart rejoices in your salvation"* (Psalm 13:5, NIV).

I had never learned how to have self-esteem; therefore I was always seeing the negative and never thinking good thoughts about myself. This deep-rooted problem prevented me from experiencing a healthy life. I've been learning a lot about self-worth and self-esteem, who I really am and how to begin liking myself. I thank God for helping me to see that our value is not in the things we do or accomplish. They are important aspects as we grow in our earthly journey, but our true value is really in God, who loves us!

We try to find our self-esteem and value through our achievements and successes, when we really need to be looking at our value in God. Our earthly achievements are good, but they're not what defines us. When we understand this, we can slowly start to move our focus from who we are as mere humans to our true value in a loving God. By learning this tool, we can be freed from things that have had negative holds on our lives. It may even help us to show healthy anger at times. God wants us to believe in ourselves. Like my adoptive dad always said to me, "Angel, God don't make junk!"

Now, take a deep breath...
and
Breathe...

8.

Are You In The Parking Lot Of Life?

"For the Son of Man came to seek and to save those who are lost." (Luke 19:10, NLT)

*D*o you ever feel stuck or lost in life? You can't seem to move forward or backward. Sometimes we're stuck, not knowing how to get out of the place we're in. We may have questions—Where do I go from here? How can I continue to grow when I have to learn to believe in myself?

Many times we become stuck in life, not knowing which way to go. If you've been through many hardships with little encouragement and few who understand where you've come from, then you may be stuck!

I've been stuck in my life's journey several times, for several reasons! At times I felt lost, and I could not move ahead. Maybe deep wounds bound me up, my attitude was unhealthy, or I just didn't understand why horrible things were happening to me. *"Though the wicked bind me with ropes, I will not forget your law"* (Psalm 119:61, NIV). It's a very stressful feeling to experience and live with day after day. I remember asking, "How long will this go on? How do I move forward from here?"

God definitely knows and understands your heart and attitude. You may feel lost or stuck in your tracks, but the Good Shepherd knows exactly where you are and what chains are binding you. Maybe your past has a hold on you, and until you clean past hurts, tragedies, and dysfunction out of your closet, stuck you will stay. It's possible to purge these toxic things from the hiding place they're locked in. The most important thing you can do if you feel stuck and don't know which way to move is to bend your knees and look up to the one who knows your every need. Many, many times I have had to do just that! God has never let me down, even in the darkest hours of my life.

While we are busy raising children, making a home, working and doing the many things that fill our lives and consume our daily time, we tend to lock away deep hurt, abuse, rejection, and dysfunction. The only way to free ourselves from all the things that bind us is by getting help and support.

Find a church to attend that offers healthy, caring support; seek out good counseling so you can have someone who cares walk you through the hurts and pains of your past. There are many good support groups today designed specifically for your needs. They will help you realize that you are not alone in your journey towards healing.

The first thing that may come out of your mouth is "I do not need counseling! I can do this myself." Many people do try self-help, and some are successful. But I have experienced too much toxicity in my life and welcome learning tools that help me to make progress towards being healthy.

The first place I look to for my help is the Lord. "*We wait in hope for the LORD; he is our help and our shield*" (Psalm 33:20, NIV). He has led me to places where I have gotten great support that, as I work hard with God's help, is beginning to free up spaces within me that once housed toxic things from my past.

It's an important thing to realize that you cannot compare your healing with someone else's. We each heal at our own speed. We each have experienced negative things to various degrees. Thus the time it takes for healing may be totally different for each of us. It's like grieving for a lost loved one; different people take different times to heal.

Find a loyal friend to confide in, someone with your values. Be very careful whom you share your story with while you are in the healing stages. If you ceaselessly search out opinions from people, chances are you will find someone who will give you the answer you want to hear. The only important opinion is God's, not others', which may lead you off the course the Lord has you on. Remember, the Lord will never get tired of hearing your cry and talking with you 24/7. "*My*

help comes from the LORD, the Maker of heaven and earth"
(Psalm 121:2, NIV).

Now, take a deep breath…
and
Breathe…

9.

Remain Humble or Stumble!

"For all those who exalt themselves will be humbled,
and those who humble themselves will be exalted."
(Luke 14:11, TNIV)

Pride! We have all experienced this destructive weapon in our lives. The Bible
clearly outlines where pride will take us, yet it
seems to be one of the most deadly tools we entertain at
the most inopportune times.

Humility! This is a tool, or attribute, that the Holy
Spirit has given us to help us remain where we should
be, with a listening and sensitive heart. When we use
true humility, we can experience positive, life-chang-
ing events. Humility is one of God's character building
tools, and it may lead us closer to Him, even in adversity.

Humility is where you take on the truth with a kind
attitude and own it. You may be wearing the garment
of truth! Demonstrating humility will move us onward,
helping us to take the less-traveled road, the one that
draws us closer to our heavenly Father. If we refuse to put
on the garment of humility, we'll have no experience but

that of stumbling! Pride can become very toxic, which in turn tears down that which God has built in our lives. So choose to wear the garment of humility. It will keep you in good standing as you progress in your life's journey.

If you plant pride in your heart, it will grow so strong that over time getting rid of it will be almost impossible. Planting humility in your heart is like ministering unto the Lord; it will lead you in His ways, and you will reap many blessings!

There are many hurting people in this world, and the only way we can truly help them is to demonstrate humility to them. For some, humility isn't even in their dictionary. They may think they have so many rights that they belong upon a pedestal, high above those who are hurting.

One thing that has brought me to humility is the path I have traveled thus far. Painful experiences and broken lives seem to bring humility faster than anything within ourselves. It may be present from not feeling good enough to belong in this life. Rejection brings us to our knees; no one does well by experiencing rejection. It's a very humbling and hard thing to live through. I have felt rejection from my abusive past more times than I would like to say. Everyone needs to feel like they belong and that there are people who love them.

Pride is just the opposite. When you are prideful, everything revolves around who you are. Your life is more important than anyone else's, and you think you can do it all better than anyone.

Humility and pride are garments in your closet. They are hanging there, just waiting to be worn. Let me caution you. Pride will bring you down from your pedestal faster than anything. God does not endorse pride. Why then is it in your closet? Well, because our closets hold both good and bad garments, and we have free choice as to which we will choose to wear. Be very careful what you choose! "*So people will be brought low and* everyone *humbled, the eyes of the arrogant humbled*" (Isaiah 5:15, TNIV).

God wants us to choose humility. It's not a sign of weakness when we wear it. Instead it makes us stronger. It's a great compass in our lives, teaching us the right way to live. "*He guides the humble in what is right and teaches them his way*" (Psalm 25:9, NIV).

"*Be completely humble and gentle; be patient, bearing with one another in love*" (Ephesians 4:2, NIV). Humility is a very good character to have. Pride is not! Wearing humility creates in us many good qualities and helps us do what God has chosen us to do. At times we make mistakes, but that doesn't mean we are failures. We aren't failures unless we actually give up trying for the Lord. Choosing humility doesn't mean you can't be proud of things in your life. It's good to feel proud of something you have accomplished. The pride God warns us about is where no one else can measure up to you, where you feel you're the only one who is right and the universe revolves around you and you alone! Those with this type of pride don't have a gentle heart and really can't be bothered spending their precious time ministering to others. We are to help and love one another. The world is a hard enough place to live in, never mind when we try to make it on our own. Pride will and does eventually bring a person down.

Pride means putting ourselves on an equal level with God. It is reserving for ourselves the right to decide what is right and wrong. Our pride is what put Jesus on the cross. "*You save the humble, but your eyes are on the haughty to bring them low*" (2 Samuel 22:28, NIV).

Again, if you have experienced pain and abuse throughout your life, you may desire to wear humility. It's what I desire. We serve a very humble God. This is proven time and again as we read in His Word how He loves us and freely gave His life for us. It is good to demonstrate humility, just as Christ did. Jesus admonishes us to "*Live in harmony with one another. Do not be proud, but be willing to associate with people of low position. Do not be conceited*" (Romans 12:16, NIV).

Humility opens the door for us to rightfully do the Lord's work, like encouraging those who are in pain and have gone through much distress and abuse. By wearing humility, we may have a better sense of perspective about ourselves and our real value. We will see ourselves on the same playing field as others.

Those wearing pride believe they are more important and better valued than others. They believe they are in a higher place, a place to judge others.

"When someone invites you to a wedding feast, do not take the place of honor, for a person more distinguished than you may have been invited. If so, the host who invited both of you will come and say to you, 'Give this person your seat.' Then, humiliated, you will have to take the least important place. But when you are invited, take the lowest place, so that when your host comes, he will say to you, 'Friend, move up to a better place.' Then you will be honored in the presence of all the other guests." (Luke 14:8–10, TNIV)

If you are prideful you will walk right up and sit by the host on presumption that you deserve this spot over all in attendance. It's better not to assume with much pride but to remain humble so that others may see your gentle, humble spirit, which glorifies the Lord. Prejudgment is the process by which you take in and interpret information about other people. Since your first impressions of others take place automatically, the prejudgment process goes on largely unnoticed by your conscious mind. Pride many times works this way. God is the only one who is in a higher place than you and me and can judge others. He is fair and judges in love. It is much better to have Him judge us!

Pride is projecting on the outside what is not true on the inside. Today, let's conquer this primary hindrance to daily success by humbling ourselves before a holy God and making things right with all those whom we have offended.[5]

"For the LORD delights in his people; he crowns the humble with victory" (Psalm 149:4, NLT). The Lord wears both pride and humility and can show love through both.

Wearing humility does not mean groveling in the dirt or being worth nothing. In fact, humility is a stronger character to wear and a very good example to others. If this is your chosen garment to wear, it shows deeply who you really are through the eyes of God. It's a daily reality check of the virtues and beliefs you uphold! *"The eyes of the arrogant will be humbled and human pride brought low; the LORD alone will be exalted in that day"* (Isaiah 2:11, TNIV).

Now, take a deep breath…
and
Breathe…

10.

Be Yourself; Everyone Else Is Taken!

According as he hath chosen us in him before the foundation of the world, that we should be holy and without blame before him in love. (Ephesians 1:4, KJV)

Who are you? Have you figured that out yet? If you have, are you happy with who you are? For some, these are hard questions to answer. For others, it may be easy to do because they have found out who they really are. How can you be yourself when you do not really know who you are in the first place?

Again, I did not feel I deserved to breathe the air; I feel it was someone else's air. I'm learning that I felt this way thus far in my life because I had not validated who I am. I did not see myself as a valuable human being. It possibly comes from all the trials and dark times I've gone through. I always felt that my identity belonged to someone else, that I'm not good enough to breathe the air, and I never felt the air I was breathing was mine. In my negative thinking I have seen others as always having it more together than me.

What do these thoughts really mean? People who feel this way have low self-esteem, problems loving themselves and problems understanding where they belong in life. These thoughts are engrained in people as small children and stay with some throughout their lives. They can snowball and become larger and more negative as they are buried inside.

I can vividly remember raising our children and struggling day and night with who I was. I never really gave myself space to realize who I was; I always felt that others were better than me. These thoughts could have come from my spirit being broken early in my life, as abuse was very prevalent. When people experience many types of abuse while trying to survive, it's hard to look at themselves with healthy, positive thoughts.

I was a very quiet child while growing up. I would seek out quiet, isolated, safe places to be. I know it was one way of survival for me. I never became aware of who I really was. I was too busy trying to hide from my tormentors. There was much fear in my life! Too many dark memories clouded my mind, and I had no time to focus on who I was. I needed to survive day by day.

I remember being on my knees one day, crying out to the Lord and pleading with Him to let me be like one of my friends. I was not happy with who I was. I wanted to be from a healthy home with love and not have to face the past that seemed to haunt me. Because of this I never felt good enough to be accepted by others. My friend was self-confident and assertive and seemed to be more in control of who she was. I saw things in her that made me question who I really was. I was tired of not knowing who God wanted me to be. I was very weary of who I thought I was and where I came from. It seemed to me that I had to work extra hard to be accepted by others. I was tired.

As I was incessantly pouring out my heart to the Lord, asking Him to change who I was, I felt a strong presence of our Lord, so loving and real, speaking to me. Jesus said to me, "There is only one of you. No one else can be you; nor can you be anyone else. I love you. I have made you who you are for a special purpose. I have given you a loving and forgiving heart after Me, which is to do the bidding of the Lord." It was so clear that beautiful day while on my knees that God didn't want me to look at others and wish I could be them. He wanted me to start the journey of finding out who I was. I have never again wished to be someone else; instead I began a journey of finding my place in our Lord.

Go to God and ask Him who you are, and He will reveal the very thing you are asking Him. He knew us even before we were born. "*I knew you before I formed you in your mother's womb. Before you were born I set you apart*" (Jeremiah 1:5 NLT).

A friend I met in counseling gave me this saying: "What's in a name? You are!" "*In him we were also chosen, having been predestined according to the plan of him who works out everything in conformity with the purpose of his will*" (Ephesians 1:11, NIV).

Now, take a deep breath…
and
Breathe…

11.

Finding Your Voice

———————

"Shout it aloud, do not hold back. Raise your voice like a trumpet." (Isaiah 58:1 NIV)

Have you found your voice? It's the ability to freely express your innermost thoughts and opinions. Is it easy for you to voice your opinion to others? Or do you just go along with others' opinions because you have a fear of saying the wrong thing to them? Do you feel confident enough to speak up? Do you believe in yourself enough to use your own voice?

If these questions are easy for you to answer in a positive way, you have found a very important thing in life: who you are as a person and that you have the right to breathe in the air and express your opinion without feeling guilty and continuously entertaining negative thoughts about yourself that tear you down. Maybe when you were growing up your parents and those who love you placed value on you; this is very healthy. If you are like me and feel a fear of speaking and using your voice, then you need to find a road to healing.

Finding my voice is one of the hardest things I have struggled with throughout my life. When I was young my right to use my voice was actually taken away from me. I was to be "seen and not heard." So I became a very quiet, withdrawn and fearful child as I learned at an early age to keep to myself. I felt it was safer that way. I was actually afraid to speak, afraid I'd be the recipient of someone's harmful anger, which caused me to live in fear.

"*You will be protected from the lash of the tongue, and need not fear when destruction comes*" (Job 5:21, NIV). I know that God has kept me and protected me, even though I experienced many types of abuse.

I never realized that we each have our own healthy voice until I was taught about it in counseling. Once I assimilated the fact that everyone has a voice and a right to use it, I was very sad and upset. I was sad because this right had been taken away from me at an early age and upset that I had to seek and learn about finding my voice at this point in my life.

When I became a Christian as a teenager, I found it easier to use my voice for the Lord and to have the strength to take a stand on what was right and wrong. However, I have always felt fear of using my voice to others in my everyday life. I continuously prayed that the Lord would give me the words to say in each situation as I walked through my journey. Having a voice and using it in a tactful way is very important in life. It is a healthy thing to have. The following is an excerpt from my journal:

> Father, please help me in someway to be able to be led by Your Spirit and to reach out to those who have been in so much pain, victimized at the expense of evil plans of men that have fallen prey to the enemy of this wounded world. If my voice could just stand for the rights of others and myself in the love of You, oh Father.

"*Evening, morning, and noon I cry out in distress, and he hears my voice*" (Psalm 55:17, NIV). Fear is a very debilitating thing to have in your life. It can seize you up and hinder your growth. There are many things we need to have a voice for in this world. Having our own voices can oftentimes protect us from evildoers and their evil plans toward us. Using our voices can also keep others from walking all over us, which I have experienced many times as the result of not being able to speak up. Our own voices can touch others' lives through encouraging words with compassion. If we can learn to use our voices in a tactful, God-given way, it will demonstrate to others that we are of value and that we are able to express our healthy boundaries to others and that their strong opinions cannot seize or abuse us. Having our own voices can help us to stand up for ourselves; no one can read a person's mind. We have to voice our thoughts and opinions to others for them to be able to know who we are and where we stand in life. Voicing our opinion helps others to find out who we really are and what we are thinking. It helps others to see through a window inside of us, learning who we really are.

"*The tongue of the righteous is choice silver, but the heart of the wicked is of little value*" (Proverbs 10:20, NIV). I am working very hard at learning how to find my voice, and I long to do it with God's guidance. I have to come to peace with the fact that the painful memories I have from childhood can no longer bind me with fears or have power over me! I am a grown woman and can make my own choices now. It's a hard thing to work through because it's the only thing I have known, and the trench is deep. It takes time to create a new, healthy path to journey on.

I have spent a lot of time pondering what I have learned, and I realize that it goes much deeper than using your voice to speak out. If you find it hard to speak what you are feeling, then you need to heal. You find out who you really are while healing the deep wounds of your past. Healing comes from God, and He can lead you to the help you need. Maybe you're like me, and your voice was hindered at an early age and replaced with ugly fear. Maybe you're shy or you don't feel good about who you are. It could be that you have low self-esteem, which prevents you from becoming courageous enough to speak. Your voice is a gift from God and should be used to encourage others, stand up for your values and integrity and express your feelings in a healthy, kind way.

It has been said that we teach others how to treat us. If we cannot use our God-given voices to help others understand who we are and what our values and beliefs are, then others will form their own opinions about who we are. If others learn that we will never speak our minds, it leaves us wide open and vulnerable to abuse from them, and some may take advantage of us.

You cannot just wake up one morning and be completely different. It takes mountains of hard work to retrain your thoughts from the negativity and fear instilled within you. But God can perform miracles, and He is capable of healing us.

I know sometimes it is hard to use our voices by saying "no" to others as we stand up for our God-given rights. I have lived a lot of my life just like this, not knowing any different. I slowly feel myself changing, moving away from this fearful thing that binds me in life, the chains that kept me in bondage. Learning the tools it takes to be able to begin baby steps towards healing and finding my voice is finally happening!

"Hear my voice when I call, O LORD; be merciful to me and answer me" (Psalm 27:7, NIV). Calling out to God for help is the most important thing we can do. After all, He made us, voice and all! Having our own voice and being able to use it in a healthy way happens when we each start to feel good about ourselves. It's the tool that can help us through our journey if used correctly.

Some people use their voices in negative ways, being mean towards others, lashing out with unfeeling words and negative talk. God never intended for us to use our voices this way. He intended for us to learn how to use our voices for positive outcomes.

"My dear brothers and sisters, take note of this: Everyone should be quick to listen, slow to speak and slow to become angry" (James 1:19, TNIV). Our voices show others what is deep within our souls. When the Lord tells us to be slow to speak, He wants us to make sure we think about what we are saying before speaking so it may be edifying to Him and all who hear. Our words have to be chosen carefully. We need to stand strong in our beliefs and who we are, keeping safe, setting personal boundaries and encouraging one another in the Lord. If you are struggling, wading through the dross of your past to get to the place without fear, to experience the liberty of using your voice as God intended, then the world will be a better place because of you!

I can say without a doubt that God can give you the strength to find your beautiful voice and learn how to believe in yourself as God intended. When I have prayed for strength and the right words to speak and the strength to do so, God has always answered my prayers, and He becomes my voice. My adoptive dad and mom always say, "If you don't stand for something, you'll fall for anything." Finding your voice is very important because it will give you the strength to speak up; therefore you are standing for something!

"I cry aloud to the LORD; I lift up my voice to the LORD for mercy" (Psalm 142:1, NIV). I chose long ago to put on

the garment of my God-given voice. As I use my voice for God's glory, it is slowly helping me to see who I really am, a child of God! You too can choose today. God loves you. *"The voice of the LORD is powerful; the voice of the LORD is majestic"* (Psalm 29:4, NIV).

Now, take a deep breath...
and
Breathe...

12.

The Building Blocks of Character

Do not be misled: "Bad company corrupts good charac-
ter." (1 Corinthians 15:33, NIV)

What is character? *Merriam-Webster Un-*
abridged Dictionary defines *character* as
"the complex of accustomed mental and
moral characteristics and habitual ethical traits marking
a person, group, or nation or serving to individualize it."
It is part of our very being.

Good character is one of the most valuable things in
life we can learn and practice from day to day. It's doing
the right thing, even if it's hard. It's knowing what the
right thing is to do, and doing it! It comes from within
our very being, from who we are. We are just babes in
arms when we are introduced to "character."

I can remember the first time I learned about character from my adopted parents, whom the Lord blessed
me with later in my life. I had always dreamed of having
a loving, caring family of my own. I continually prayed
for this, and the Lord answered my prayer. I could not

ask for better parents. I have been blessed! I was legally adopted in 1993. I became a part of a wonderful family, and I deeply thank God for this. It has filled an empty, lonely place in my heart. It has helped me feel as though I belong. I have learned so many things about character. *Character* is also the word used for someone who is acting out a part on television or in plays and theater productions, but in the reality of life, character is the molding and making of who we really are from the inside out.

As a potter molds and shapes his clay to make a pleasing work of art, we mold character within us. As we journey down the road of life, we pick up characteristics that mold and shape our very being. Character displays our true values. It all starts on the inside and is reflected to others on the outside.

If you can, imagine a closet before you. As you open the door you gaze upon many articles of clothing. Each piece of clothing wears a tag labeled with a characteristic, good or bad. It is up to you which article you choose to wear. As a small child others may choose for you, so you have no choice. Hopefully they are articles that are good to wear.

As we mature, it is our choice whether to keep the characteristic that we are subjected to or drop it. It's like putting on an article of clothing. We try a characteristic on, and if it fits we usually keep it. There are both good and bad characteristics to choose from. Which kind we are in contact with usually depends on our surroundings. But, the bottom line is, each individual has a free choice to decide which characteristics they will pick up and wear or pass by in their journey here on this earth.

When I was a small girl, someone dared me to go into a drugstore and steal some mascara. Challenges do spark my interest; besides, I thought it was a way of making others accept me. I took the challenge to heart and did it. I actually stole a package of mascara to prove to the one who dared me that I could do it! Everything was going well until I reached the front door of the drugstore to leave. I heard a man's voice calling out to me, "Stop!" I stopped dead in my sneaky tracks! I knew stealing was wrong, but it was a minor thing to me in that moment. At that time, the feeling of belonging was a higher priority for me.

The police were called, and I was reprimanded for my wrongdoing. Honesty is a characteristic, and at that place in my journey I threw it off so I could feel acceptance. The sad thing is that the very one who dared me to prove my allegiance by betraying the characteristic of honesty was nowhere to be found when I was caught! I learned that day that throwing away a good character for someone's approval dragged only me down, not the one giving the dare.

It's very hard to build good character and trust back up once they have been worn and then discarded. The good news is that it *is* possible to do! I did pick up that discarded characteristic once more and tried with all my heart to always wear it. You see, the damage it brought was hard to turn around. Trust was broken with those who knew me, and for a long time when I went into that drugstore the owner never took his eyes off me. I think if we can learn from our mistakes the characteristic we make allegiance with is stronger. God knows we are only human, and His grace is always waiting for us. He is the one who created "character" so that we, His children, can choose for ourselves to wear garments made out of good character. Pleasing our Father in heaven is really the most important goal we should have. Others let us down because they are mere human, but God is the author of good character!

As a teacher, it is very important for me to try to incorporate good character choices within my curriculum. Each Monday I introduced a healthy characteristic and read a story related to that characteristic to my students. I felt that incorporating these healthy characteristics into my curriculum would help my students learn and gain better life skills. These character sketches used animals to demonstrate certain characteristics. Here are just a few: patience, integrity, joyfulness, determination, decisiveness, deference, security, wisdom, tolerance, honor, cautiousness, endurance, initiative, diligence, loyalty, forgiveness, determination, and dependability. Character is very important to have and wear in our lives!

Abraham Lincoln said, "Reputation is the shadow. Character is the tree." Our character is much more than just what we try to display for others to see, It is who we are even when no one is watching. Good character is doing the right thing because it is right to do what is right.[6]

Our Father in heaven is a God of good character. There is a quote I love to read from time to time: "You cannot change the people around you, but you can change the people you choose to be around" (Anonymous). Choosing to wear articles of good character will bring many blessings into your life as well as to others around you.

Choosing to find good friends in our life will definitely help our healing from the offenders we have encountered thus far. Good character shines through us. It is worth more than pure gold. Many years ago I began to immerse myself into wearing garments of good character, and it has held me in good stead.

Just as we need to learn how to incorporate good character within our lives, we also need to take off those bad influences learned as a child. At first it may feel very awkward to do, but the longer we move towards and walk in this new path, the more it feels like it belongs to us. Don't be hard on yourself; it takes time to build new and healthy paths towards healing in your life.

Now, take a deep breath…
and
Breathe…

13.

Integrity and Values

May integrity and uprightness protect me, because my hope, LORD, is in you. (Psalm 25:21, TNIV)

Kings take pleasure in honest lips; they value persons who speaks what is right. (Proverbs 16:13, TNIV)

What is integrity? It is when you have strong moral values and principles, such as being honest, having strong moral principles and good moral uprightness. It is also doing what is right when no one is looking!

It is important for each of us to incorporate integrity into our lives, making a strong effort to walk and talk integrity in our journey each day. "People who demonstrate integrity draw others to them because they are trustworthy and dependable. They are principled and can be counted on to behave in honorable ways even when no one is watching."[7]

There is one person whom I have learned a lot about integrity from, and that is my adoptive dad. He is such an inspiration and mentor to me as he demonstrates integrity and good values each day of his life. I thank God for the family my Father in heaven chose for me when I was a young adult. I love my dad and mom more than I can say. They have endeavored to show me love, integrity, good values and compassion from the day the Lord brought me to their home. My brothers and sisters mean the world to me, and I am thankful for their love and acceptance. I saw what my dad had, and I wanted it so very much. After I began to live with them in 1977, I prayed so hard that I could learn and strive to be like my dad. I am very thankful to God for instilling these characteristics in my heart. It's not always easy to stand strong, but life is much better when we wear the garments of integrity and good values. It can only be done with the help of our Lord. Thank You, Father. "*The integrity of the upright guides them*" (Proverbs 11:3, NIV).

What are values? Values are leading principles that guide us and motivate us as we move through life. A value is a principle or quality that we want to stand for and how we want to behave on an ongoing basis. Values are freely chosen. What is important to each of us is our personal code of values. Values are things you really need in your life to be true to yourself. In the value-focused life, the emphasis is on living by our values in each moment. If we could roll our values together, they would be our convictions, ethics and beliefs. Do you know where they come from?

Some of your values are inherited; others are learned from parents, teachers, and very important people in your life. Our environment also sways our values. Our values can definitely come from God as well. Our values may change as we grow older. Roy Disney said, "It's not hard to make decisions when you know what your values are."

Now, take a deep breath…
and
Breathe…

14.

Who's Your Daddy?

One God and Father of all, who is over all and through all and in all. (Ephesians 4:6, NIV)

The Lord became a resident in my heart when I was a teenager, although I always had a longing to know God, even as a small child.

I saw an angel when I was a small girl and going through the fire of unhealthy things as others made unhealthy choices that impacted me. This vision has never left me! The angel was peeking through a cloud, looking down at me. She was a young angel, almost like a cherub, with the deepest blue eyes and curly blonde hair. Her beautiful face was so kind and illuminated! I knew at that moment that God had His angels watching over me. Even through all the darkness I endured, God has placed in my heart a deep love for Him and others.

Maybe you wonder if there is a God and why He would allow such horrible things to happen in this world. It takes more love to allow us to learn from our own choices than to make all our choices for us. Taking away our freedom of choice would cause us to never learn or grow and thus would be unhealthy. God does not intend for us to be puppets on strings.

He could stop bad things from happening in a heartbeat. Why doesn't He? Where is He when tragedy strikes?

He is there with a broken heart just as you are, and He does care for you. He's not going to make people do what He wants them to do. He gives us free choice, and it grieves His heart when we choose things that are not right. You see, free will is what God has given us each and every day. And many times people make bad choices with their free will instead of good choices that please God and uphold integrity. Even though you have made a wrong choice at one time or another, God is waiting for you to call to Him so He can help you right the wrong that has been done. *"You are forgiving and good, O Lord, abounding in love to all who call to you"* (Psalm 86:5, NIV).

I gave my heart to the Lord at a Billy Graham crusade one summer evening. There were thousands of others there packed in the bleachers on that promising warm evening. I just couldn't leave without having the chance to invite God into my heart. I felt a strong calling in my heart, so on this very evening I started to make my way to the front where Billy Graham was. That night I earnestly surrendered my heart to our Lord. When I went to bed that night, I felt the precious love of God even more! He placed within my heart the following poem, which was a great help to me throughout the rough paths I was being led on:

Thank You, Father, for this day,
May I show You love
In everything I do and everything I say
Please help me, Lord, to praise You all day long
And help my faith and trust stay strong.
For You are the bright and morning star,
The God of ALL things near and far.
My whole life, Lord, I owe to You,
For You changed it completely and made
me new.

Since I can remember, I have loved the Lord in my heart all of my life. In past days you could still read Bible story books in the library at school. I would seek them out, and I really learned a lot from reading them! It was as if I had a deep hunger for the things of our Lord and just couldn't get enough of reading about God. After giving my heart to our most precious Lord, I knew my life would never be the same.

Giving your heart to the Lord does not have to be done in a huge stadium with thousands of other people. It can be done alone or with another Christian helping you. You can humbly and sincerely ask God to live in your heart anywhere; He will hear you, and your life will never be the same as you begin to walk with Him. There still may be very hard times, because the world is quickly moving away from God's values. The best part about being a Christian is that you are never without God's help and love, even when you feel you are. No matter what your journey is on this earth, with God all things are possible! When you are in the midst of trials the Lord is right there in the trenches with you, supporting and loving you.

Being a dedicated Christian is hard work. The most important thing we can do is to strive to do God's will with a humble heart, the purpose of our journey. He is our Father, God, friend, help in times of trouble, teacher and leader, and most importantly he is our daddy who loves us.

Many times when I have gone through numerous trials I have wanted to climb up on my daddy's lap in heaven and find refuge, comfort and strength there. It's an awesome thing to do, because His unending love surrounds you while you feel safe in His arms. It was hard for me at first because I never had a daddy when growing up, so it was very uncomfortable to desire this. I had to step out of my comfort zone, get past my fear, and reach out my arms to my loving Father in heaven.

Growing up, I spent a lot of time in foster homes. Unfortunately, the homes I was placed in never seemed to work out. One of the worst ones I endured was with a family that already had six children. I was not treated well, and thus I continued to feel unwanted. I remember the dysfunction of the home, which included many immoral activities. One day I walked in on the foster mother and others and caught them doing something I shouldn't have seen. I was therefore placed in a locked room in the back the house for what seemed to be forever. I ran away when one of their daughters forgot and left the door un-locked after bringing food to me. I ran to the police sta-tion, and they sent me to live with my biological father, whom I really did not know.

I wasn't there long before my father, who was a truck driver, forced me to go on one of his trips haul-ing something. I know now he had a motive behind his plan for me. Once we were in the middle of nowhere he pulled the truck over and forced me to swallow a couple of pills. He then forced me to get into the sleeper part of the truck. My personal boundaries were crossed and my innocence was stolen from me, and once again I experi-enced abuse on this horrible day. How could someone do these things to his own daughter? I remember scream-ing, but no one could hear me in the isolated area he had driven to. I still hear his sick voice and his words to me: "I am only doing what every father does to teach his daughter how to be a woman in life." I remember being so very fearful of him because his temper was full blown aggression. I felt so ashamed, blaming myself while ex-periencing fear, sadness, hurt and shock!

Once we returned to where he lived, I tried my hard-est to seek help, but no one in this family believed me! I was told that I deserved everything I went through and it was never to be talked about again. I started to believe that the things being yelled at me repeatedly were true, that I deserved everything that I went through. I was no good and probably asked for what I got. I was told that I would never amount to anything anyway! I experienced a lot of rejection and became, in my thoughts, the bad person. The types of things that I lived through were to be kept behind closed doors. I put on the garments of "guilt and shame" and have worn them for most of my life. I had drawn the conclusion that many of those I had contact with were there to hurt me and take whatever they wanted from me. I learned early in my life that I could not trust anyone! Why was I even on the earth, breathing air?

As a child I knew what beatings were like. I would have to go out into the backyard and pick a willow switch, which would be used to whip me until I could no longer stand. As I grew older I began to rationalize that maybe it was just a way for my mother to relieve her anxiety in her own journey, as she was very young when her responsibilities came along. The deep pain has been unbearable at times throughout my life, and I know I have blocked much out in order to function. All I knew was that I had great fear of the woman who gave birth to me, and thus I could not trust her. When pain is a great part of your life, trust does not come easy for anyone.

These were the years when many things were being formed within me as a small child growing up. The message I learned again was "I do not deserve to breathe the air I breathe." I didn't think I was good enough.

Again, depression has been a hard struggle at times throughout my life. It was much more prevalent when I was experiencing difficult trials of rejection, abuse and sickness. Many times I wanted to curl up and never wake up again, because my journey in life was just too hard. There was nothing stable about my young life. Many adults freely abused me, invaded my privacy and then discarded me to survive on my own. Many crossed my personal boundaries, and my innocence was stolen from me many times at an early age; I could trust no one.

I slept in churchyards at times, not having a pillow to lay my head on. I didn't know where my next meal was coming from. I felt as though I had fallen through the cracks of life and was not supposed to be here on earth. I can remember never wanting to go home when I had one. My trust had been deeply broken, causing me to be afraid of everyone. I used to pretend my life was different, that someday I would be rescued and have a good home. (Praise God for giving me a loving home now, later in life!) The Lord was the one who rescued me—maybe not in the way I pictured it by taking me out of the situations I lived through, but He walked with me through the fires instead.

In 1977 I was blessed to meet a family that eventually became my loving, caring family throughout the rest of my life. I was legally adopted as an adult in 1993 by my caring God-given parents. This healed a part of my life; I finally had a place where I really belonged. Everyone needs to belong somewhere, feeling like they have a family that needs them. Even though my prayers were answered and I was so very happy, my next challenge was to learn to adapt to a healthy environment. Everything seemed so foreign to me. It was unlike anywhere I had ever lived, and in my heart I wanted it so much! God gave me the strength to move on.

I can honestly say that I have never been mad at God for my toxic, tumultuous life; through it He has helped me learn how to lean on Him. Again, the Lord gave me the most precious gift we could ask for in life, and that was a loving heart for Him and the ability to forgive. That does not mean it has always been easy, because the pain at times has been unbearable. Knowing God is with me is what keeps me hanging on, putting one foot in front of the other each day. I didn't know anything about Jesus or God, but I always had a longing in my heart for Him. He has given me a loving heart even while my journey has been so hard.

My life began to change slowly after I invited Jesus to live in my heart. I longed to do His will and share His salvation and love with others. It has been a long journey towards healing.

I thank God that today there is more awareness and support groups for those like me who have survived things that make God weep. Finally things are brought out into the open and more people are made accountable for their wrongful actions toward other human beings. There is help out there today, which is a wonderful breakthrough for many hurting people.

Again, I am not ashamed to say that I have made the choice to receive counseling so I can heal and recover from my tumultuous life journey. There are things I am learning now that I had never known and had never been taught while growing up. The healing process has begun, and if I told you it was easy, I would not be telling the truth! There are days when I would prefer to pull the covers above my head and retreat. So as I ask myself, "Who's my real daddy?" the answer for us all is our Heavenly Father, Lord of all things. He loves us with all His heart, and we are very special children belonging to Him.

Many mistakes are made here on earth. In order to release the bonds of past abuse, I have had to forgive those who hurt and abused me growing up as an unwanted child, tossed to and fro. Even though it is hard for me to disclose parts of my life and its ugly chains that bind, with a gentle heart I speak, using my voice God has given me, in hopes of reaching out in the Lord to be a help to those who have traveled down the same atrocious path.

The more I let the Lord into my life, the closer I feel to Him and the more I begin to internalize that He really is my daddy in heaven. I am learning that even though I was deeply hurt by my real father, God is my daddy who cares for and loves His children each and every minute of every day! I am learning not to be afraid of Him, trusting Him more and more. It's a safe and deep loving care He has for us, unlike those who strive to hurt us.

Take some time out of your day, which is a blessing unto God, and sit with your daddy, your Father in heaven, who loves you. Enjoy His gentle love for you. Get to know Him, and laugh a lot; it is healing. "*He will yet fill your mouth with laughter and your lips with shouts of joy*" (Job 8:21, NIV). "*A cheerful heart is good medicine, but a crushed spirit dries up the bones*" (Proverbs 17:22, NIV).

Now, take a deep breath...
and
Breathe...

15.

Forgive and Forget: Can You Have One Without the Other?

Therefore, my brothers and sisters, I want you to know that through Jesus the forgiveness of sins is proclaimed to you. (Acts 13:38, TNIV)

The answer to this question is, Yes! Forgiveness is a tough concept to understand for many, especially those who have been deeply hurt and abused by others. There is a process you can walk through that can heal your heart. This process does not usually happen overnight. You have to learn about forgiveness and how to use it to start the deep healing.

> FORGIVENESS. To be clear, the purpose of forgiveness is not to absolve someone of the sin(s) committed against you; but to free yourself from the pain and the anger that is keeping you stuck. When you forgive, you are better able to let go of the past and keep moving forward with your life.[8]

Jesus is the best example for us in learning about forgiveness. He was abused and rejected by men many times, yet he gave His life on the cross for us. He forgives those who have wronged Him, even those who have wronged others. *"In him we have redemption through his blood, the forgiveness of sins, in accordance with the riches of God's grace"* (Ephesians 1:7, NIV).

Forgiveness does not mean that we can forget the wrongs directed toward us by others. You cannot turn back the clock and redo what has happened, but you can reach for the tool of healing through forgiveness. Why would you want to forgive someone who made your life miserable by inflicting pain, abuse and hurt upon you? You may have asked yourself, "Do I really have to forgive that person who offended me? How can I do this? How can I ever forget the deep pain I have endured from my abusers?" We cannot forget the deep scars of pain and abuse. *"But if you do not forgive others their sins, your Father will not forgive your sins"* (Matthew 6:15, TNIV).

The good news is that the abuse we have encountered can be looked upon in a positive light eventually, when we've healed enough. We can choose to learn from the painful, negative experiences by letting them teach us, by trying not to be the victim again and not to victimize others.

When we forgive those who hurt us, we're not condoning their actions. We may never be able to forget, because scars will always be there within us. But as time goes by we may think of our scars less often. When we decide to forgive others for their actions toward us, it does not mean they are not responsible for their actions. They have to make amends and peace with their past.

Forgiveness is not a form of self-sacrifice. We have to be honest with ourselves about being ready to forgive. When we are, then it is true forgiveness. To say we forgive someone and go away with bitter, hateful feelings while holding a grudge and wanting revenge is just being a martyr. True forgiveness cannot be forced. It should happen naturally as we decide to confront our painful past. *"For if you forgive others when they sin against you, your heavenly Father will also forgive you"* (Matthew 6:14, TNIV). God freely forgives us of our sins, and He wants us to forgive others as well.

Forgiveness can heal old wounds, which is what God desires for us. It comes while in the healing process. We experience it when we stop expecting those who hurt us to suffer or pay for what they did. When we are ready to forgive, it brings with it feelings of acceptance and health and provides a freedom for us. As we begin to experience good self-esteem, forgiveness is easier to do.

When we have forgiven someone, it helps us to recognize that we do not need to harbor resentment, grudges, self-pity or hatred. If we desire to punish the one who has hurt us, forgiveness helps us to accept that nothing negative we do to the abuser will heal us. Holding grudges and entertaining bitterness is very unhealthy, and we will never be able to let go of the offense. Instead it will weigh us down in our journey. Choosing forgiveness breaks the cycle of pain and abuse. If we choose not to forgive those who have caused us much pain, we use our energy to nurse unhealed wounds instead of to do God's will. If we want to move on in our lives, we need to forgive! Forgiving the people who hurt us frees up our energy to experience a more healthy life. It takes the weight off that we have been carrying.

God desires that we choose true forgiveness so we can completely dedicate our whole selves unto Him to do His will. We can use our experiences to do good by empathizing and helping others who are going through a similar situation and need someone to help them.

True forgiveness cannot be forced upon us. We have to grow into it, especially when there are triggers that go off from time to time and remind us and take us back to the pain, which never seems to goes away! A trigger is like having a flashback of something that happened to you in the past. It may be a remembrance of a painful or traumatic event that you have lived through. Different things trigger different people. It may be feeling rejected, being blamed or devalued as a person, feeling inadequate, or encountering certain smells and sounds.

If we choose to hang on to the hurts others have done to us, we will not be able to progress forward and lead a healthy life as God wants us to. Our hearts will be so full of bitterness and pain from our abusive past that we feed those negative thoughts. We will begin to harbor toxic bitterness that fills our hearts with deep-rooted weeds that eventually take over our lives. Martin Luther

King Jr. said, "He who is devoid of the power to forgive is devoid of the power to love."[9]

I have experienced a tremendous amount of abuse in my life, and for most of my life I was told that forgiveness goes along with forgetting. "You are supposed to forgive and forget, then move on!" How can anyone forget the deeply painful, abusive, hurtful things encountered in life? We are not God, so therefore we do not have the ability as He does to throw our pains in the *"land of forgetfulness"* (Psalm 88:12 NKJV). We can however look to our Lord for healing. He will help us move forward, and in time the scars may diminish.

Forgiveness is a commitment to a process of change.[10] It takes time. Everyone's healing time is different; depending on the offenses they have endured. An abusive incident leaves a huge open sore on the body of the victim. This open sore encompasses pain, swelling, bleeding and much more. Sometimes it's so deep that it needs stitches. If left unattended, it becomes an abscess that does not have the ability to heal on its own. It may remain as an open sore for many years, and the pain may be unbearable. Then the one suffering the aftermath of abuse may be stuck at a certain place in life with no ability to move on.

Forgiveness can be very difficult, especially if the person who has offended us doesn't want to admit their wrong. We are not responsible for the offender to ask for forgiveness; that is not the point. Forgiveness is more about how it can change our lives. It can take away the power of the other person who continues to manipulate our lives.

This is where forgiveness comes in to play. Notice I did not say "Forget." Genuine forgiveness is more for the victim of abuse than the abuser. The abusers will have to make a conscious decision to choose forgiveness with their free will; it's not our responsibility!

> Forgiveness is a decision to let go of resentment and thoughts of revenge. The act that hurt or offended you might always remain a part of your life, but forgiveness can lessen its grip on you and help you focus on other, positive parts of your life...Forgiveness doesn't mean that you deny the other person's responsibility for hurting you, and it doesn't minimize or justify the wrong. You can forgive the person without excusing the act. Forgiveness brings a kind of peace that helps you go on with life...Letting go of grudges and bitterness can make way for compassion, kindness and peace.[11]

Again, forgiveness does not mean that you are letting the offender off the hook for his or her actions, and it doesn't minimize or justify the wrong. You can forgive a person without excusing the act. Forgiveness brings us peace that helps us heal in our life. It sets us free from the bondage of that hurt or wrongful act. When we choose forgiveness it can free us of carrying around the shame, guilt and hurt we wear. It frees up space in our hearts so we may fill it with healthy things instead of holding on to the hurts others have done to us. It does not mean we will never be reminded of the hurt or feel the pain again. Prayerfully in time those open wounds will heal, but unfortunately we are still left with a scar. Hopefully those scars can remind us to use our sad memories for good, to help someone else out who is walking the road we have walked.

There are many hurting and lost souls in this world, and before I began to travel this road I was one of them. I still have such a long way to go, and it may take my whole life on this earth; only the Lord knows. We cannot change other people and what they decide to do, but we can change ourselves so we can eventually experience a healthy life, which can bring compassion, peace and kindness. "We need to be the change we wish to see in the world."[12]

Now, take a deep breath…
and
Breathe…

16.

Letting Go!

I will maintain my righteousness and never let go of it; my conscience will not reproach me as long as I live. (Job 27:6, NIV)

Letting go…for some, this is a very misunderstood statement. Letting go of something that's not healthy is an important step to follow but is often taken out of context. To let go of a situation may be easily understood by some but a daunting nightmare for others. There are things in our life that we do not want to let go of, just as Job speaks of in the preceding verse. He wanted to hold on to his innocence that others were trying to entice him to let go of, proving his trials were from his own sins.

There may be many different reasons why we need to let go of something. Generally it's because it's not healthy for us. Letting go of things that are unhealthy helps us to walk forward and grasp hold of healthy things that will help us to live in a healthy environment.

The following is a poem that I received in my counseling class:

To "Let Go" Takes Love

To "let go" does not mean to stop caring; it means I can't do it for someone else.

To "let go" is not to cut myself off; it is the realization that I can't control another.

To "let go" is not to enable, but to allow learning from natural consequences.

To "let go" is to admit powerlessness, which means the outcome is not in my hands.

To "let go" is not to try to change or blame another; it is to make the most of myself.

To "let go" is not to care for, but to care about.

To "let go" is not to "fix," but to be supportive.

To "let go" is not to judge, but to allow another to be a human being.

To "let go" is not to be in the middle arranging all the outcomes, but to allow others to affect their own destinies.

To "let go" is not to be protective; it is to permit another to face reality.

To "let go" is not to deny, but to accept.

To "let go" is not to nag, scold or argue, but instead to search out my own shortcomings and correct them.

To "let go" is not to adjust everything to my desires, but to take each day as it comes, and to cherish myself in it.

To "let go" is not to criticize and regulate anybody, but to try to become what I dream I can be.

To "let go" is not to regret the past, but to grow and live for the future.

To "let go" is to fear less and love more.[13]

ROBERT PAUL GILLES

Hanging on creates a very heavy toxic weight that disrupts our walk with the Lord. There are so many things that can weigh us down in life, and I pray that each one of us will draw close to God to seek His will and direction for us. The Lord is there to carry our heavy load and help us let go of the things that weigh us down. The most important thing in life is to be where God wants us to be and to travel down the path He has chosen for us. Sometimes it is so very hard let go and let God. It may be the hardest task we achieve. If we cannot let go it has the potential to seize us in our tracks! Letting go of an unhealthy situation is an important factor in growth. Some may be able to accomplish it with ease, while the others find it a continual battle that promotes mental warfare. It may seem like an enormous task, but if not completed, progress and growth in life may be hindered.

Letting go brings the healing and forgiveness needed to walk a healthy journey. I carried a lot of baggage that I didn't need to; it weighed me down, creating depression many times, which led to thoughts of not wanting to carry on. It became too hard! But I have begun to learn that letting go does become easier when practiced. I have also noticed that it makes a big difference in relationships with others, especially those close to me.

If you have to let go of someone or something, you need to practice caring assertiveness with love. It may be for their best interest, because there are things we cannot change. It's also practicing how to stand up for yourself and make healthy choices.

Letting go of the heavy weight of our toxic past is a very important thing to do. It helps us remain healthy, physically, mentally and emotionally.

We have to learn to let go of our grown children, letting them make their own choices, whether they please us or not. They too have free will and are responsible for their choices and the consequences that follow. We have to let go of things in our lives that are toxic for us to continue to be a part of.

I have been in many situations where I have had to forgive and let go in order to maintain my health and well-being. I have had to let go of a child who has chosen a path that isn't healthy. It was like someone was ripping out my heart! I have had to let go of toxic behavior in my life to maintain a peaceful home so I could continue to grow through my journey.

Letting go of something is one of the hardest things you will ever have to do. If it's concerning a child or young adult child, it can tear your heart up, but at least it will not enable them, which may hinder their growth and maturity as self-reliant adults. They will be able to stand on their own two feet and travel the road of their own journey with God's help.

We can use the analogy of a mountain climber. When people make a goal to hike up a steep trail or climb a mountain, they take as little as possible, just the necessities, to keep their load as light as possible. If the load becomes too heavy, the climb is hindered and the ascension to the top is much harder. In fact, they may not even be able to reach the top without letting go of that which weighs them down. It will weigh them down, thus hindering their task to reach the top! We want to make sure that we are ready and available to do the things we are called to do at the time we are summoned to do the will of God.

Letting go of something that holds worth to you or something you have become accustomed to is very hard to do, especially if you know in your heart the Lord has asked you to do so. I know this from experience.

I completed my teaching degree as an adult and taught as a teacher for approximately thirteen years. Due to many circumstances I had to go on stress-sick leave. I had dreamed of getting my degree all of my life and finally was able to achieve it with the help of God. The grown-ups in my life throughout my childhood always told me that I would never amount to anything, ever. I guess I was determined to prove those naysayers wrong. When I was sick and no longer able to teach, I was crushed. My life had been "interrupted." I felt as though

I was lost, with no purpose anymore. I love teaching, and I will always thank God that I was able to reach this dream. I know in my heart that the Lord was leading me in a different direction at this time. It has been very hard to try to understand, but in my heart I know I just need to let go of the things that have hindered my walk with the Lord. I know that I need to trust the Lord and keep my true faith that He knows the path I will walk. I try to be ready when He calls.

Since my life has taken a drastic turn, interrupted with physical illness and the need to work through the hidden things in my heart, I am looking to the Lord for what He wants me to do now. I have found it very hard to "let go" of one of the most important things in my life for now. I know within my heart that if I carried this heavy load with me of not wanting to let go of teaching and the toxic things of my past that are hidden under the iceberg of life heavily weighing me down, I will drown and never make it to the glorious mountain peak. Letting go is one of the most important things to practice that brings forgiveness, freedom and health to one's soul.

During counseling, as I became more aware of the things I needed to let go of, I wrote the following poem. It's about the little girl who has forever hung on, not wanting to let go but continuing to fight for my survival. I am a grown woman now and have free choice. I want to let go and free this little girl who was frightened and alone living inside of me. She will always be a part of me because she is me! My burden will be lifted. My hopes and dreams are to realize that I am out of the danger I was once in and that the little girl can be set free to replace sadness with joyfulness!

I am a survivor of the dark, toxic journey of my past and now am learning to heal all that is buried deep within.

LITTLE GIRL

There is a little girl within me,
She never goes away,
A little girl who carries much fear and pain.

Her large blue eyes are soft and saddened,
This clearly can be seen.
When you look deep within them,
They are crying, "Please…please help me!"

She hides in corners, closets, and underneath the beds,
Behind open doors she silently stands,
Breathing shallow breaths,
It's quieter that way,
Bringing safety, keeping her from becoming one's prey.

Hiding, running like a frightened deer,
Fighting for survival each day.
Tearstained face and moist blonde hair stuck to her face.

She has to hide maybe just one more day,
Except…
For the days she is locked away in the attic,
dark and dreary there.
Will this nightmare ever end?

Years go by, this little girl survives,
Now she's a grown woman today.
But she still feels the little girl's pain inside.

It's as if she hides within me still
Running from the previous pain.

I have to let you go now, little one,
You'll always be my memory.
What you don't know is…YOU have been set
free!
No more hiding, afraid of becoming someone
else's prey,
They are ALL gone, no more pain!

You made it…SURVIVED…the help of God
with you each day.
Now it's time to play and experience,
The good things life can bring your way![14]

I am sure the family I was born into had many toxic
issues; otherwise I would have been welcomed instead
of hated.

Inner peace is found when you endeavor to change yourself and not others who have hurt you. Do it for you. You deserve to be healthy!

"*My eyes are ever on the LORD, for only he will release my feet from the snare*" (Psalm 25:15, NIV). To release something is to "let go" of it. If we strive to keep our eyes on the Lord and follow in His paths, He will certainly help us as we endeavor to let go of unhealthy things that weigh us down so we can climb to the mountaintop with Him and reach the peak!

Today it's time to let go, let go of anything that's bringing you down. Don't let negative circumstances deter you from the wonderful things life has to offer. If it's not uplifting it's not worth it.[15]

Now, take a deep breath…
and
Breathe…

17.

Positive Thinking vs. Negative Thinking

Jesus knew what they were thinking and asked, "Why are you thinking these things in your hearts?"
(Luke 5:22, NIV)

sick man was being lowered on his mat through the rooftop so Jesus could heal him because there was such a large crowd gathered. Jesus knew what the Pharisees and teachers of the law were thinking. He wanted to know why they were starting to speak negatively. Negative talk spreads like wildfire! Negative people need drama like it's oxygen. Try to stay positive and take their breath away!

Positive thinking is healthy, while negative thinking is very toxic for us. It's a learned behavior that is very connected to who we are and how our journey in life proceeds. Negative thinking is embedded in a child's life and is like a bad weed; it can spread very quickly and is hard to get rid of! The more we entertain and pay attention to our negative thoughts, the more they grow. We all know how hard it is to keep weeds from growing. If left alone, the weeds will eventually consume and choke out anything that is good. We need to challenge the negative voices and say "No!" This has to be tended to each and every day on a continual basis to prevent the toxic effects such thoughts bring into our life.

My thinking has been, for the most part, negative, unfortunately. By entertaining negative self-talk I am being hard on myself. This self-defeating behavior has robbed me of many healthy experiences, bringing much pain and negativity. It has embedded within me the belief that I'm a worthless person, not good enough for anything. But I have made a serious attempt to turn my negative thinking around so I can think good things about myself with God's help.

Positive affirmations are essential in our lives each day to help us heal and gain self-approval, and it's also very important to act upon the positive words that we speak to ourselves. As we become familiar with our self-worth we learn to recognize and accept our responsibilities in life. We learn to own up to the fact that we, with God's help, are in control of our attitudes, reactions and sense of worth.

Eleanor Roosevelt once said, "No one can make you feel inferior without your consent."[16] We must be careful to not let others and our circumstances serve as the source of lowering our self-esteem. If this happens to you, you may become stuck in your journey.

It is very important that we take ownership for our behavior. Using blame to cope with our life problems alleviates our need to look at ourselves and change our own behavior. Blaming others can tend to keep us stuck with our negative feelings, Blame implies that something or someone has the power we lack. We should be taking ownership of our own actions so we are not left to feel we lack the power to make the choices we need to change our life. "Avoid being a martyr; the responsibility to move on as a strong, whole person rests with you."[17]

Our self-talk is very important. We can continuously wear the garment of negative self-talk, which is demeaning, or we can decide to learn how to wear positive self-talk, which brings healing within us and eventually gives us the power to change and heal, led by our Lord.

You need to wear the garment of positive self-talk. Make an effort to give yourself some positive self-talk each day. The following exercise is very difficult to do, especially if you've never done it before. Use a mirror to do this, anywhere you can be alone with yourself. Speak positive affirmations to yourself, which should include statements like the following:

I am a great person.
I am special.
I am lovable.
I am wonderful.
The Lord loves me.
Others love me.

Place encouraging Scriptures where you can see and read them each day! There are many more affirmations you can say as well. By practicing this you can slowly begin to change the way you actively take part in refocusing your self-talk. And in time you will be speaking positively instead of negatively. It will eventually help you see and believe that you have value and deserve the air you breath. You do matter, as much as every person around you!

When you catch yourself speaking negative things to yourself, *stop*! Step back and look at the situation. Would you talk to your best friend this way? Would you speak to someone you dearly love this way? If the answer is no, you need to change your self-talk from negative to positive. If you continue negative self-talk, even if it is the way you were taught, this could eventually spill over into others' lives around you.

We should strive to use "I" statements rather than "You" statements. Using "I" statements when communicating with others takes the blame out of our comments. It tells the other person how we really feel without blaming them. It is taking ownership and responsibility for our own actions. In contrast, using "You" statements quickly places blame on the other person, which may cause resentment, defensiveness and resistance. An "I" statement is easier to hear because there is no blame attached to it. When using an "I" statement we own and describe our feelings. In a "You" statement we judge and blame others for our feelings. Here's a simple formula to use for an "I" message: "I feel _____ when you ___ because _____."[18] This is what it may look like after you fill it in: "I feel better when you are kind because I do not feel fear." If the statement used "you" instead of "I" then it would be blaming the one you are speaking to, such as, "You feel more arrogant than me when you are not kind to me because it makes you feel in charge."

It feels very uncomfortable doing this at first, but it will eventually become more comfortable. Before you know it, it will become a healthy part of you! You then will be on your way to becoming a real friend to yourself, learning about who you really are in a positive light. God made you special!

We could look at negative self-talk as a deep trench we have worn down. It can be very daunting to try to picture climbing out of that trench we have become so comfortable in.

I grew up with negative thoughts thrown at me all the time as a child and young adult. It's hard to find value in yourself when negative talk is all you hear. I did not learn how to be a positive thinker until I met and became a part of a family that opened their home to me in love. My God-given dad is still to this day a wonderful example to many. In his daily life, whether a good day or troublesome, my dad always tries to look at the positive side of things. I admire him so much for this example he is to all of his children and those God brings into his path. Thank you, Dad, for being such an inspiration to me, your adopted daughter. I love you, Angel!

Positive thinking can be instilled in children's lives. This is very important, because children will have many years to have this healthy value permeate their beings. They will learn at an early age that they deserve the air that they breathe each day because they have value. Those close to them valuing who they are creates healthy people as they grow up.

This was only a dream for me while young. No matter where I looked, I could not find this healthy family. God blessed me as an adult by blessing me with my family.

Finally, brothers and sisters, whatever is true, whatever is noble, whatever is right, whatever is pure, whatever is lovely, whatever is admirable—if anything is excellent or praiseworthy—think about such things. (Philippians 4:8, TNIV)

The Lord encourages us to think about good, positive things, and this includes you! He is helping me learn how to stop negative thoughts about myself. By His grace He helps me to replace them with positive thinking. I am nowhere near complete healing in this struggle with self-harm, but I am learning how to take baby steps.

Please, do not lose hope; these healthy things can be learned as an adult. It is just much harder. If children are taught when young to believe in themselves and are shown that they have value, what a precious gift they have been given!

Positive thinking comes with feeling good about who you are. Remember, Healthy skills take time to practice. Do not be hard on yourself!

Now, take a deep breath...
and
Breathe...

18.

Is Your Atmosphere Protecting You?

Keep me as the apple of your eye, hide me in the shadow of your wings. (Psalm 17:8 NIV)

What is our atmosphere? It's what surrounds and protects us here on earth. It is only the thing that keeps you from being burned to death every day, helps to bring the rain that our plants need to survive, not to mention it holds the oxygen that you need to breath. Essentially, the atmosphere is a collection of gases that makes the Earth habitable.[19]

We all desire protection each day. Our atmosphere is our protection while we live here on this earth and walk through our journey God has prepared for us. I am not a scientist, but I do know how very important it is to each of us to have this protection. God is our atmosphere; He is our safety, the one who provides our air each day and keeps us alive.

The people and the environment we each live in and around are considered to be part of our atmosphere. I did not want to experience rejection anymore. I did not put two and two together to realize rejection was present in the first place as well as fear. I did not have a healthy self-esteem to voice such an important thing that was going on behind closed doors, the inside story.

If you can relate to this story, then it is most important for you to find your voice and get some help for you and your children. The good news is that God can help you, and when He does your atmosphere can change to a safe one. God does not want to see His children suffer in pain. He loves us. If asked, He can be your voice to find help so you can cling to Him, so your atmosphere can be a safe and healthy one. You do not need to continue in the pain you are experiencing.

The following lyrics describe the environment of someone who is suffering, yet no one hears her plea for help. I was this woman at one time and was afraid to speak up for fear of rejection from the life I had worked so very hard to attain.

INSIDE STORY

It's Sunday morning, it's 10 a.m.
The congregation is gathering in
And she smiles like the rest of the women
and men
But inside, her heart is breaking.

'Cause her man showed his rage, again
last night
but, like a martyr though, she didn't fight
And the wounds he gave her, she was able
to hide
She comes around for a reason.

And she sits in the crowd alone with the pain
she hides so well
Wishing someone knew the inside story, she's
so afraid to tell
She needs someone to talk to, to see the pain
that's in her eyes
She needs someone who will listen
And to see through her disguise.

Its been awhile, since she believed
That she's worth more than the pain he leaves
And she doesn't think much of the woman
she sees
When she looks into the mirror
Now she's afraid of the man she loves
She blames herself for the things he does
Oh! How she wishes he'd be like he was
Back when his touch was tender.

And she sits in the crowd alone with the pain
she hides so well

Wishing someone knew the inside story, she's
so afraid to tell
She needs someone to talk to, to see the pain
that's in her eyes
She needs someone who will listen
And to see through her disguise.

Now they're singing a closing hymn
Soon they'll be saying the last "amen."
And maybe next Sunday she'll come again
But she'll come around for a reason.[20]

Steve and Annie Chapman

Using your voice is very important so if needed you can find positive help and your atmosphere can begin to be restored to a healthy one. "*The LORD protects the unwary; when I was brought low, he saved me*" (Psalm 116:6, TNIV). Look to the Lord, and He will listen, hear and save you. I know because He did this for me. You are very special to our Father in heaven.

Even though others may not see it or believe us, God knows our hearts and what goes on behind closed doors. We all need structure and boundaries in our life to feel safe. The first step to healing is to admit the unhealthy environment or atmosphere we are living in to someone who can help. "*Hear me, O God, as I voice my complaint; protect my life from the threat of the enemy*" (Psalm 64:1, NIV). We all deserve to live in a safe and healthy atmosphere.

Sometimes fear and hope that you can change the other person is what you focus on while feeling afraid that you may lose all that you have worked so hard to build. The truth is that we cannot change others; that's their choice to make for themselves. In the meantime, find safety, and take what is hidden and bring it out into the open. *"Keep me safe, LORD, from the hands of the wicked; protect me from the violent, who devise ways to trip my feet"* (Psalm 140:4, TNIV).

Now, take a deep breath…
and
Breathe…

19.

Loving Yourself

Whoever does not love does not know God, because God is love. (1 John 4:8, NIV)

Do you love yourself? Do you know how to love yourself? Do you feel guilty when you spend any time for yourself? There is a difference in loving yourself and being stuck on yourself.

I have been learning about a very important tool to healing, and that is "self-care." What is self-care? Self-care is when you take responsibility for your feelings, thoughts, actions and choices. Self-care is about learning to set boundaries for your own good, saying no, asking for help when needed and valuing your own welfare with God's help.

Self-care can be as little as listening to music you like, taking a bubble bath or taking a few moments for yourself so you can regroup your thoughts and show yourself you are valued. More importantly, it is showing the Lord how much you appreciate His love for you.

It is very important to learn self-care through the steps of our healing. As we take steps toward recovery, the goal is balance. Most of us reach that middle ground by exploring the peaks and valleys in our healing. There will be triggers along the way that may be very painful to walk through, but it is our desire to be able to recognize and work through our relapses. We learn much from the valleys and the peaks within our journey toward recovery.

Being stuck on yourself or thinking of just yourself all the time is just the opposite. It is where you do everything just for you, whether or not it hurts others and brings them pain. You do not care as long as you are thinking of yourself, forgetting the needs of others. This is not the Lord's way for us. He wants us to care for and encourage one another.

There's a point in our recovery where we need to stop taking care of everyone else's problems and ignoring our own, to take care of who we are, thus, self-care. This does not mean that we should never care for others or help them; it means that we have to begin to make room in our lives to practice self-care. By doing this we are showing ourselves and God our appreciation for who we are.

I have never learned how to practice self-care or love myself until I became aware of it in counseling class. I always had the negative talk that "If you do this for yourself, you are being selfish." I always strived to please others before myself, until there was nothing left of me, and I usually ended up physically sick. In my thinking it was the right thing to do so others would like me. I see now that I talked myself out of self-care many times. In the first place, I learned at an early age to not like myself or give any positive time to myself. I think I was really my first enemy.

It all begins at an early age when as a small child you have reinforcement of who you are and how you are valued. If those around you are imparting negative thoughts about you, then you will learn to feel very negative about yourself and who you are. On the flip side, if you are receiving positive affirmations about who you are from others, then there is a good chance you will grow up liking who you are and feeling comfortable about practicing self-care.

Here is an excerpt from one of my journals that I wrote a while ago:

I am learning so much about myself and how I have not been healthy throughout the years because of my tumultuous journey here on earth. I long for healing in this area of my life. Things I should have learned, I did not. There was no one in my life to teach me as a child. So, my normal was different than what a healthy, secure, upbringing should be. Instead of experiencing security, I lived in fear. Instead of learning trust, I learned to withdraw and trust no one. Instead of learning I was a good person, with a special purpose, I learned shame, guilt and rejection with no self-confidence. Instead of learning to care and look after myself because God made me special, I learned to take my frustrations and anger out on myself in negative self-talk. Instead of learning I was worth something and loved, I learned to dislike myself and feel worthless. I learned that I do not deserve to breathe the air we have been provided with on this earth. I have learned from a small infant to dislike who I am, never feeling good enough. All of these engrained things that have been woven deep within me has been my bondage, the chains that bind me. Oh how deep within my heart I long to be set free from the horrific experiences of my past and present trials that are shutting down my physical and emotional being. How does one assimilate and embrace this new understanding when all I have ever known is the opposite of healthy?

I thank God that I have come a long way since I wrote this in my journal. I have learned about how important it really is to love myself and practice self-care.

We each have the right to do healthy things for ourselves. Learning to do these things gives us more strength to give to and help others. It is extremely important to learn how to love ourselves. At the core of our well-being we should find self-love. If we never learn how to love ourselves it can be very debilitating . It can cause us to have self-doubt and uncertainty, which may turn into depression and self-hatred, emotionally crippling us. God is the one who created us for His pleasure and made us who we are. If we do not love ourselves, then we are rejecting what God has made in His image. *"Through him all things were made; without him nothing was made that has been made"* (John 1:3, NIV).

Next time you talk to yourself, step back and think about what you have said. We are usually the hardest on ourselves as we judge and criticize ourselves harshly. Sometimes we treat ourselves far worse than we treat others. When we learn to speak to ourselves with positive self-talk, our self-esteem goes up! So one of the most valuable activities that we can partake in is self-care. If we learn to love ourselves, as Christ wants us to, it helps us to take care of others in a world that can be hard at times. Sometimes as we go through the struggles of learning to love ourselves, it can feel like all we have is our breath. It's important to take deep breaths when focusing on learning to change ourselves.

We need to learn to treat ourselves with love, respect and kindness without feeling guilty. *"Because Your loving-kindness is better than life, My lips shall praise You"* (Psalm 63:3, NKJV). Kindness is caring enough about others and ourselves that we treat them and ourselves with gentleness, graciousness and generosity. Kindness is a characteristic of God.

Criticism never changes a thing. Refuse to criticize yourself. Accept yourself exactly as you are. Everybody changes. When you criticize yourself, your changes are negative. When you approve of yourself, your changes are positive.[21]

"Love is patient, love is kind. It does not envy, it does not boast, it is not proud" (1 Corinthians 13:4, NIV). "Be gentle with yourself. Be kind to yourself. Be patient with yourself as you learn the new ways of thinking. Treat yourself as you would someone you really loved."[22]

The opposite of loving yourself is self-hatred. "Self-hatred is only hating your own thoughts. Don't hate yourself for having the thoughts. Gently change your thoughts."[23] Again, it takes different times for different people to heal.

Loving yourself is an unconditional process. It means you accept, appreciate and celebrate all of who you are. *"My command is this: Love each other as I have loved you"* (John 15:12, NIV). If you have no problem loving yourself, you should be very thankful to God, because this is such an important step in leading a healthy life.

By learning to love yourself you are actually validating that you are meant to be here, that you do have value in God, your daddy and father. You are a very special creation of God, and He has blessed you with the air you breathe each and every day.

I am still learning to love and put value on myself without feeling guilty about doing so. With God's gracious help I feel as though I am making progress, no matter how small at times!

I remember always taking care of others, because I never learned that it's important and healthy to look after myself, to place value on who I am, a child of God. In counseling, we were always told at the end of the class to go home and practice self-care, to take the time to do something very special, to be kind to ourselves, because it's not easy to work on the deep-rooted trials of our past.

Sometimes it felt as though my brain was smoldering. It is so very hard to dig deep within myself to get rid of the pain that encompasses me each day. Many times it is painful to get to the root of our deep-seated hurting experiences we have held on to. Many times we had to process the fact that we needed to "let go" of the negative thoughts and behaviors learned as a child. It is very hard to love yourself if you really never get to know who you are. The good news is that if you are willing to work diligently, to take full ownership and to get out of the worn trenches of your negative thinking, then you can begin to love yourself!

Again, one of the healthy tools I use in my road to recovery is journaling my feelings, which helps me to express my inner feelings. No one ever has to read it; it is between me and God.

God loves you, and He always will. You are His creation. Despite the direction your life has taken you, beyond your control, you can still learn to love yourself, as Christ wants you to. You are His beautiful creation, and He cherishes you. You can begin today to choose the right path to healing. *"Let love and faithfulness never leave you; bind them around your neck, write them on the tablet of your heart"* (Proverbs 3:3, NIV). I pray that God will help you to understand the great love He has and always will have for you!

Now, take a deep breath…
and
Breathe…

20.

Love Never Fails

We love Him because He first loved us.
(1 John 4:19, NKJV)

This is my very favorite chapter, "Love Never Fails." When I was just a small child I know that God placed a great love within my heart and a deep desire to know Him better each day, basking in His love. I have a deep love for people, especially those who are hurting. I know, as was said earlier, that God weeps when He sees His very own walk through pain and tribulation because of man's free will to make their own choices. Usually it involves someone who has no control over the others' actions and choices. We can choose to continue as victims and carry the pain around with us while it eats away at who we are, or we can look to the Lord to help us forgive, let go and learn how to use our voices so we may someday be able to help someone else who is going through the same pain. God does not want His children to suffer at all, and it creates sadness as He weeps.

Even though I have experienced many types of abuse that have left me depressed, hurting, sad and physically ill, where I wanted to run and hide, I believe with all my heart that that's not who I really am. In order for me to learn who I really am I need to reach out to God, as I have throughout my life, and with needed help, empty the toxins of hidden abuse and deep hurts. Sometimes it feels like I am chipping away at it very slowly because it will not pour out on its own. It has made a deep impression and many scars on my life. I know with God's help I can heal. The scars may always be there as a reminder of where I came from to keep me on the right track.

When Jesus rose from the dead and met with the disciples, Thomas was not there and later did not believe the other disciples' report. Later Jesus came again and said to him, *"Put your finger here; see my hands. Reach out your hand and put it into my side. Stop doubting and believe"* (John 20:27, NIV).

Jesus was rejected by men, dragged, beaten, kicked, mocked and eventually hung on a wooden cross to die. He did this for you and me. This is how much He loved us, and He still does today. When He rose from the dead and met Thomas, He used His scars to prove to Thomas that it was really Him. As Jesus is the Son of God, it would have been an easy task to heal those scars, but He did not. He knew that the scars would prove to His followers that it was their Master, who suffered so badly. We also sometimes go through traumatic things in our lives, and these things usually leave scars. The point is that hopefully in time we can forgive those who have hurt us, but we do not have the power to make our scars go away. Jesus knows our weaknesses and how hard it is for us to believe some things; this is why He wore the scars, so others would know without a doubt that He is our risen Savior!

The horrible things that some have gone through in life over time can be healed, but the scars are ever present to remind us of the dark times and hopefully be used of God to help those in need. If someone has told you, "All you need to do is forgive and forget—never to be brought up again, thrown into the sea of forgetfulness," remember, we are not God. He can throw things into the sea of forgetfulness because He is God. We are mere humans, and we look to God for our healing and love.

Many people have been healed through God's grace and love, but our scars remain to remind us. It is possible for God to take away our scars. I do believe in miracles, but He is the only one who can heal in such a deep way if He chooses. I think our scars may be left behind to remind us where we have been and the life lesson we have learned from it. If we go through life hiding our hurts, abuse and sins under a rug, then there will be a time when we are going to have to deal with it and find healing. The rug can only cover so much! We have to get rid of our hurts and pain that we're harboring so we'll have room to grasp ahold of the healthy things God has in store for us.

There is a time very soon where we will have to get rid of the dross and toxins and replace them with God's love and guidance. "*For whatever is hidden is meant to be disclosed, and whatever is concealed is meant to be brought out into the open*" (Mark 4:22, NIV). God does not want us to hide things in our lives anymore. He knows us inside and out.

May we each have a desire to deal with the things that are hidden in our lives so we can be healed and begin our journey into the kingdom of God. Healing only begins when we clear away (with God's help) everything that is diseased and injured. "*Love does not delight in evil but rejoices with the truth*" (1 Corinthians 13:6, NIV).

The most beautiful people we have known are those who have known defeat, known suffering, known struggle, known loss, and have found their way out of the depths. These persons have an appreciation, a sensitivity, and an understanding of life that fills them with compassion, gentleness, and a deep loving concern. Beautiful people do not just happen.[24]

It is my prayer that the healthy tools mentioned in this book will be of help to those who are looking for the path to healthy healing in their life. These healthy tools can help begin our healing as we endeavor to take this chosen journey, and remember, it is not over until you breathe your last breath! Love never fails. God is our Healer, Comforter, Savior, loving daddy. He is the very life we breathe each day. So it is my desire that those reading this book will think seriously and make a commitment to choose the road toward healing. We all know that if you have experienced abuse in your life, the only way to find the long, hard road to recovery is through our Lord Jesus Christ. As long as we cling to Him, He will our healer.

Do not be discouraged. The Lord sees your heart and has walked in your shoes of pain and abuse. It may take quite a while to heal for some, but remember it is *not* impossible as a child of God. Though the road may be hard, *do not* give up! Praise be to our God, who loves us unconditionally. *"Love never fails"* (1 Corinthians 13:8, NKJV).

Now, take a deep breath...*you* are a survivor...
Know in your heart *you* are His child...
Now, take a deep breath...
And
Keep Breathing...

Endnotes

1. Michael W. Smith, "Breathe," on *Worship* (CD), Reunion Records Inc. (released Dec. 1, 2000, published 2001).

2. "How We Breathe," Cedars-Sinai, http://www.cedars-sinai.edu/Patients/Programs-and-Services/Lung-Institute/Patient-Guide/Anatomy-of-the-Lungs/How-We-Breathe.aspx.

3. Dave Sper, "Choices and Consequences," Our Daily Bread, December 28, 2011, http://odb.org/2011/12/28/choices-and-consequences/. Taken from Our Daily Bread, © 2012 by RBC Ministries, Grand Rapids, MI. Reprinted by permission. All rights reserved.

4. WordNet Search, s.v. "dignity," http://wordnetweb.princeton.edu/perl/webwn?c=0&sub=Change&o2=&o0=1&o8=1&o1=1&o7=&o5=&o9=&o6=&o3=&o4=&i=-1&h=000&s=dignity.

5. Bill Gothard, "Conquer the Greatest Sin," Daily Success, http://mailings.iblp.org/getresponse/output/index.php?day=5.

6. "The Meaning of Character," *What Is Character?*, http://www.character-training.com.

7. Susan M. Heathfield, "What Is Integrity—Really?" Human Resources, http://humanresources.about.com/od/Trust/g/what-is-integrity.htm.

8. Alex Blackwell, "What Are Your Values? The Most Important Values to Live By," The Bridgemaker, http://www.thebridgemaker.com/what-are-your-values-the-most-important-values-to-live-by.

9. Martin Luther King Jr. (1929–1968), minister, civil rights activist, "Forgiveness," Values.com, http://www.values.com/inspirational-quote-authors/1390-Martin-Luther-King-Jr-.

10. Mayo Clinic staff, "Forgiveness: Letting Go of Grudges and Bitterness, " Adult Health, Mayo Clinic, http//www.mayoclinic.com/health/forgiveness/MH00131.

11. Ibid.

12. Mahatma Gandhi, Arun Gandhi's summary indirect quotation in "Arun Gandhi Shares the Mahatma's Message" by Michel W. Potts, in *India—West* [San Leandro, California] vol. 27, no. 13 (1 February 2002) A34.

13. Robert Paul Gilles, "To Let Go Takes Love," *Thoughts of the Dream Poet: vol. 1* (1997), http://www.soencouragement.org/to-let-go-takes-love.htm.

14. I wrote this poem.

15. Unknown, http://www.searchquotes.com/quotation/Today_it%27s_time_to_let_go,_let_go_of_anything_that%27s_bringing_you_down._Don%27t_let_negative_circumsta/387363/.

16. Eleanor Roosevelt, *This Is My Story* (1937), http://www.goodreads.com/quotes/11035-no-one-can-make-you-feel-inferior-without-your-consent.

17. Greg Ican, Lois Wade, et al., eds., "How to Build Self Worth," WikiHow, http://www.wikihow.com/Build-Self-Worth.

18. Langley Memorial Hospital Mental Health Counseling, used with permission.

19. Jerry Coffey, "What Is the Atmosphere?" http://www.universetoday.com/54760/what-is-the-atmosphere/#ixzz2Sf134RAF.

20. Steve Chapman, Copyright © 1987 Dawn Treader Music (SESAC) Shepherd's Fold Music (BMI) (adm. at CapitolCMGPublishing.com) All rights reserved. Used by permission.

21. Louise L. Hay, "Do You Love Yourself?" Heal Your Life, http://www.healyourlife.com/author-louise-l-hay/2013/01/wisdom/personal-growth/do-you-love-yourself.

22. Ibid.

23. Ibid.

24. Elisabeth Kubler-Ross, *Death: The Final Stage of Growth* (1975), http://www.ekrfoundation.org/quotes/.

Watch for other titles by Anne A. Koltes, coming soon.

Notes

Notes

Notes

Notes

....
....
....
....
....
....
....
....
....
....
....
....
....
....
....
....
....
....
....
....
....
....
....
....
....
....
....

Notes

Notes

Notes

....
....
....
....
....
....
....
....
....
....
....
....
....
....
....
....
....
....
....
....
....
....
....
....
....
....
....

Notes